I0829556

Between Eternities

© 2024
Heinz G. Ross
Gold Coast
Australia

Between Eternities

by
Heinz G. Ross

2024

Copyright Notice

ISBN: 978-0-6459281-4-3 (Hardcover)
ISBN: 978-0-6459281-5-0 (e-book)

BISAC code:
POE000000 (POETRY / General)
LCO000000 (LITERARY COLLECTIONS / General)
LAN005070 (LANGUAGE ARTS & DISCIPLINES / Writing / Poetry)
POE023010 (POETRY / Subjects & Themes / Death, Grief, Loss)
POE023070 (POETRY / Subjects & Themes / War)
POE023030 (POETRY / Subjects & Themes / Animals & Nature)
SOC045000 (SOCIAL SCIENCE / Poverty & Homelessness)
FAM001010 (FAMILY & RELATIONSHIPS / Abuse / Child Abuse)

Disclaimer

The contents of this book, titled 'Between Eternities,' are intended for entertainment, creative exploration, and intellectual stimulation. The author would like to provide the following disclaimer to ensure clarity and understanding for readers:

Fictitious Nature: The stories, characters, events, and scenarios portrayed in this book are primarily products of the author's imagination. Any resemblance to actual persons, living or dead, or to real events is purely coincidental. The author has taken creative liberties to construct fictional narratives for the purpose of storytelling.

Literary License: The author has employed literary license throughout the book. Certain words, phrases, or expressions may be used metaphorically, symbolically, or in a manner that deviates from their literal or conventional meanings. Readers are encouraged to approach the text with an open mind, recognising the author's intention to evoke emotions, provoke thought, and create a unique literary experience.

Satirical and Tongue-in-Cheek Content: Some sections of the book may include satirical elements, humour, or a 'tongue-in-cheek' approach to certain subjects. Readers should interpret such content with an understanding of the author's intention to entertain and engage in social commentary.

External Links: In some cases, the book may include links to related videos or audio content. These external links are provided for informational purposes and further exploration. The author does not guarantee the availability, accuracy, or content of these external resources and encourages readers to exercise discretion while accessing them.

Individual Interpretation: The themes, ideas, and messages conveyed in 'Between Eternities' are subject to individual interpretation. Readers are encouraged to engage with the text critically and form their own perspectives based on their personal experiences and beliefs.

The author appreciates readers' engagement with the book and encourages an open dialogue about its contents. However, the author cannot be held responsible for any personal reactions, opinions, or actions arising from the reading or interpretation of 'Between Eternities.'

Trigger Warnings: The author acknowledges that some readers may have personal experiences or sensitivities related to topics explored in 'Between Eternities.' While efforts have been made to handle sensitive subjects with care, it is essential for readers to prioritise their emotional well-being. Trigger warnings have been included to highlight sections that may contain content that could be distressing or triggering. 'Between Eternities' contains a wide range of creative works and diverse content covering a broad range of the human condition, including grief, trauma, loss, suicide and others. Please proceed with self-awareness and considerate care for your emotional well-being. Some of these may offer some comfort to a reader whist another reader may be triggered by the same. One needs to realise that even the song of a nightingale can trigger traumatic experiences of the past in some individuals. To make this work safe for any reader Trigger Warnings are included in the Table of Contents and the relevant Titles, such as:
Hush (Trigger warning: Child abuse). Please seek professional guidance and care if such subject are causing you discomfort.

By continuing to read 'Between Eternities,' readers acknowledge and accept the sensitivity warnings and the author's efforts to provide a safe reading experience.

Table of Contents

Preface

'Between Eternities' is my 15th book. This anthology presents a unique collection of poems and lyrics, spanning the vast spectrum of the human condition. It seeks to embrace universal emotions that bind us all. Within these pages lie verses that echo the joys and sorrows, hopes and fears, dreams and regrets that colour the canvas of our lives.

Each word is carefully crafted, imbued with raw emotions. From the delicate hues of love's tender embrace to the darkest corners of human suffering, 'Between Eternities' ventures to explore the intricate fabric that connects us as sentient beings.

While words have the power to heal and inspire, they can also evoke memories of pain and trauma. This collection does not shy away from addressing the complexities of life; as such, it embraces sensitive subjects that may be distressing to some readers. To ensure that readers approach these pieces with mindfulness, trigger warnings have been thoughtfully placed where appropriate.

Like the ebb and flow of tides, this book oscillates between moments of contemplation and moments of catharsis. It invites readers on a journey that traverses the vast landscapes of the heart, mind, and soul. Through the intertwining verses, readers may find solace in shared experiences, forging connections with both the familiar and the foreign.

As readers embark on this poetic odyssey, may they find moments of introspection, revelation, and empathy. Let the words within 'Between Eternities' be a mirror, reflecting the myriad facets of existence, and an embrace, welcoming readers into the shared human experience.

In addition to the poetic offerings, this collection provides supplementary insights. Within this collection, many poems are accompanied by details revealing their date and place of origin, providing a portal into the diverse landscapes that sparked their creation. Some poems have transformed into musical compositions, and the included chord progressions underscore this transition. Where possible, direct links have been included to these works while leaving room for potential additions in the future, accessible through my channel link. Beyond mere reflection, the anthology serves as a revelation, encapsulating moments suspended in the dimensions of both time and space. This work includes photographs and AI generated images.

In all forthcoming works, I will unequivocally employ the name Heinz G. Ross, adorned with my unique HR logo, to differentiate myself from the numerous authors and artists who share the name Heinz Ross, while also emphasizing my location as the Gold Coast, Australia.

Heinz G. Ross

Links

Website: http://www.heinzross.com

Email: mailto:info@hrexposure.com

All Videos: Youtube Video link

Music Videos playlist: Music Videos

Music & Video: reverbnation

Music (Audio only): https://heinzross.bandcamp.com/

Music (Audio only): https://soundcloud.com/heinz-ross

Poetry / Lyrics

Alive in all we are

This lake contains the breath of our ancestors,
contains the blood of our kind,
harbours the remnants of our forebears.

We and this lake are relatives.
This lake and so many others have links to us.
Every cloud contains a part of our history.
Each played a part, however long ago,
that in time allowed us this view.

And in the ground beneath our feet,
our brothers' soil in kind.

Our heritage is in front of us,
around us, in us,
alive in all we are.

Video: https://youtu.be/LhJwQ1wuwWk

All that I own

The spring claimed that it owned the creek,
the creek claimed rivers, and the sea,
the banks and shores amazed,
'Without us, where they'd be?'
All raised their voice,
each claimed their own,
'cept one with many names…
'What do you own?' they questioned.

'All that I ever own is I,
was born with all I had,
and when I die each part of it
I will be giving back.'
'All that you own you are?'

 The rivers fell as banks gave way
and ground beneath drained sea.
…when earth looked in its pockets
found soil and seeds and streams,
found bones and rocks and golden locks
and as it always knew…

'Then take a look inside yourself,
you, one with many names,
is not all that you are of me,
all that you own on loan?'
…then asked the falling drops of rain,
'Where will you go?'
'We're coming home.'

Video: https://www.youtube.com/watch?v=bTw2wkdVXpM

Holy ground

The soil hid under rusting sheets
no blade of grass to see the sun
the battery's poison content seeps
no seed to stand a chance

The debris fades in bleaching sun
no fruits that it can grow
footsteps not found
on wreck-strewn ground
abandoned lay as waste

Look at the scars you have me bear
not mirror of my soul
the shame not mine, but I'll endure
as caustic acid soaks the ground
burns all which once had life

Discarded remnants won't fuel growth
but fruitless barren soil,
use have I none of what you brought
digest I try but can't make ore
nor sand from glass of other shores

Have you forgotten who I am?
...the blossom from the burning ground
the root that brought you healing,
I fed each plant you ever ate,
my breast not failed in feeding

I am the dusk, the dawn, the day
I am the night of calming break,
the oceans, lands and mountains high
and all that dwell within

I am the aggregate of all
since time saw light of day
and everything your eye can see
your then, your now, your history

If I'm not holy ground in life
how can I be
when you're in me
be place of final rest?

Video: https://youtu.be/OA4ckZfUBFE

Thanks for the sandwich (Trigger warning: Suicide, abuse)

Yes, it's cold in winter.
A bit of a breeze chills you to the bone,
but with enough rags and cardboard you get by.
The bins will keep the wind off you.

In summer I sleep in the park.
It's better then, 'cept for the 'skitoes.
Here they rob the poor for a fix,
same as everywhere else.
When the nutters need money,
they start to hassle you.
If you got nothing,
they beat the living crap out of you.
It's tough. What are you writing all that down for?
Whatever.

See the one on the bridge?
She's looking down into the water.
She swings forth and back,
and it looks like any minute she's going to jump.
Every other days she has a go.
She's had enough.
She's been trying to kill herself so many times.
Perhaps her young ones still hold her back,
but no doubt, one day she'll do it.

First she was abused at home,
then her mum kicked her out when she was 14,
that's when she started living in the streets.
She's got a couple of kids, you know.
Two boys and a girl.

She's not even 27 yet,
but she is very tired.
Tired of living.
I feel sorry for the kids though.
She grew 'em up under a plastic sheet.
The youngest is just 4.
The streets are the only home they know.
It's not right, but what is.

Each parent is looking just after their own.
Those that start behind the 8 ball,
give theirs a legacy of doom,
that continues throughout generations.
It's a vicious circle.

What's it to you anyway?
Perhaps Jacky told her the bridge is the way to go.
You got to overcome the fear.
He knows of many ways to go
when you had enough.

Someone suggested CO2, but it's painful.
Jackie said you need argon, nitrogen, or helium,
to stop the pain.
But it's difficult to set up.
Get it wrong and you're a veggie for the rest of your days.
That would be real misery.

Another said, cutting is quick,
you need to cut along it, not across,
and not on the wrist, it'll take forever.
It makes a mess either way.
I know of a 10-year-old,
she used a rope, she did it first go.
Jacky knows a lot on the subject.
It's not my thing. I wait for my number.

Nice Merc you got there.
I had a Merc, 10 years ago,
then my business collapsed.
Too many overheads.
I had the hounds at the door.
Now I don't have a door anymore.
I've been living the streets for seven years now.

The only overheads I have now,
is this fig tree.
Next week I'll lose it.
The city wants to cut it down.
Looks like you got it made,
as long as you can keep the hounds at bay.

Why did you come here for?
Are you looking into your crystal ball,
your mirror into the future?
I talk too much.
Pay me no mind.

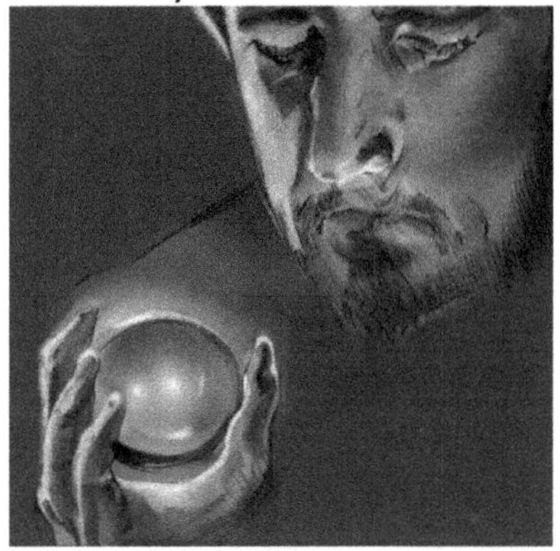

I've seen many come and go here.
You get chased from one place to another,
and you move on.
At first you carry your pride and self-esteem in a plastic bag,
then you lose it.
Some people spit at you, give you dirty looks.
Are we the vision of their own fear?
I grew up believing,
that the value of human dignity,
is unimpeachable, the highest order of the land.
Well, a long time ago, that we're all equal.
T J must have had a sense of humour.
I used to believe in tomorrow,
but I've learned since,
it never comes.
You are constantly being judged.

They want you to move on, to go away.
What's a home? I can't remember any more.
Her kids certainly don't know what a home is, 'cept the sheet.
This is all they know.
In time they become wise and street-smart.
At least they're not dreamers.
There are many little ones, here,
too many.
When they're in front of some shop window,
everybody sees them and wants them to move.
But yeah, what can you do?

There are old ones too.
The frail, the sick, the junkies,
pick any label.

Some are in pain, depressed, and many are disillusioned.
I guess It all depends, on how much pain you can bear.
Just one thing is certain:
next week there will be more.
But why am I telling you?
Anyway,
thanks for the sandwich,
appreciate it.

See you.
Video: https://youtu.be/9L5JSJheBSk

Thank you (Trigger warning: Loss)
Cambodia

Time may come soon
or sooner,
when all that I was given spent

no strength then left to blink my eye
no breath to say my last 'good bye'
perhaps I'll mess my pants

I know that you will carry me
wrapped in clean sheets
sad-faced, you'll do,
and many wonder
where you find the strength
to lift my tiny bundle
of sore-marked skin and bones

each bundle adds
to what you've carried
day after day,
for months and years

my final breath
be 'thanks' to you
for all that you have given

you called me Mister since day one
and Miss, my sister, barely two
each body placed upon the twigs
found time of calm and soothing
between the pain they had endured

each hand you held,
each name you called
found rest
because of you

08 May 2012

(I wrote this when I saw a picture of Wayne Dale Matthysse carrying the remains of a child to the twigs. I sent it to him.)

Video: https://youtu.be/BKS9WE41fkQ

The video is in English language, with English, Khmer and German subtitles. The text in the following page is in Khmer language. Khmer translation by: Chea Arun

'Thank you' relates to 'Wat Opot', a children's orphanage, now better known as a children's community for vulnerable children, near Phnom Penh, Cambodia. Nearly 500 people have passed away from AIDS/HIV or related illnesses at Wat Opot since 2001 (recorded in 2012). The following Video provides a better understanding of what is written here.

Related Video (made in 2012):
https://www.youtube.com/watch?v=JKI1AwcsNy8

សូមអរគុណលោក

(as previous in Khmer)

ដង្ហើមចុងក្រោយ អាចខិតមកដល់
ក្នុងពេលខាងមុខ ឬ ក្នុងនាទីដ៏ខ្លីបន្តិចទៀតកនេះ
កាណកម្ដៅងកាយ នឹង
ចិត្តរបស់ខ្ញុំត្រូវបាត់បងសូន្យទៅ ។

ខ្ញុំគ្មានសូម្បីតែកម្លាំង ពព្រិចភ្នែក ។
គ្មានទាំងដងផ្ដើមដួយឲ្យខ្ញុំអាច ពោលពាក្យថា "
លាហើយ " ជាចុងក្រោយបានទៅៀកផង ។
ខ្ញុំប្រហែលជានឹងរាក ប្រទ្បាក់ខោក់មិនដឹង ។

ប៉ុន្តែខ្ញុំដឹងច្បាស់ថា លោកនឹងបិត្រកងថែទៅ
គ្របដណ្ដប់វុំកាយខ្ញុំ ជាមួយនឹងក្រណាត់ថ្មីស្ងាត
ប្រកបដោយទឹកមុខស្រពាប់ស្រពោន ។
លោកនឹងផ្ញើដូច្ធោះ ។

ហើយអ្នកខ្លះពិតជាឆ្ងល់ថា
តើលោកបានកម្លាំងពីណា អាចដួយឲ្យលោក
លើកបិត្រកងថែវាងកាយ ដំស្ពាំងស្មរបស់ខ្ញុំ
ដែលពេញដោយកមរមាស់ ដណ្ដប់ផ្លឹង ។

អ្នកជម្ងឺម្នាក់ៗ រូបបន្តែមនឹងអ្នកជម្ងឺដទៃៀទៀត
លោកផ្លាប់បានផ្ទាក់ថ្មមថៃទៅ រូចហើយ
មួយថ្ងៃហើយមួយថ្ងៃទៀត ហួតរាប់ខែ ឬ
ក្នុងករណីយខ្លះ រាប់ឆ្នាំ ។

ដផ្ដើមចុងក្រោយរបស់ខ្ញុំ គឺជាសេចក្ដី " អរគុណ "
ចំពោះលោកដែលបានផ្ញើ អ្វីៗទាំងអស់ដល់ខ្ញុំ ។

លោកបានហៅខ្ញុំថា លោក " Mister " ហើយ
អ្នកនាង " Miss " ឬួនស្រីខ្ញុំ
សូម្បីតែនាងមានអាយ
ទើបតែមិនទាន់បានពីរឆ្នាំផង ។

អ្នកជម្ងឺម្នាក់ៗ ដែលលោកផ្ងេកលើត្រែ
បានរកឃើញភាពស្ងប់ខ្លះ នៅចន្លោះ
ភាបឈឺចុកចាប់ ដែលគេកំពុងប្រឈម ។

ដែនិមួយៗដែលលោកកាន់ នឹង
ឈ្មោះនិមួយៗដែលលោកហៅ
បានរកឃើញសន្ដិភាព
ក់ដោយសារតែសេចក្ដីមេត្ដា នឹង
ករុណារបស់លោក ៕

só (Trigger warning)

Perhaps a word of warning is appropriate, as the subject is a bit different, but it too is part of the human condition. The idea came from reading some very abusive and rude comments about a site, and another comment stating the opposite. The comments became a trigger. It is written in very simple style, trying to be inoffensive.

The midnight goddess, teens,
18 years old, so many, bold,
with childlike face of innocence
weave dreamlike promise, so it seems,
at 22 considered old

Some sell their youth, of faultless beauty,
come join me, I'll show you all
could you please help, I'm really broke
need 100 bucks, perhaps some more,
give you free voucher for a dream

Lonely old fool knows all too well
no chance on earth, perhaps in hell
I give you all if you'll be mine
How much you got? You got me thinking

I'd be in heaven if I could
just hold your body in my arms
trade all my vouchers for a kiss
my hand just once, to feel your oh...

Oh darling friend, you are so cute
just swipe the card for 100 bucks
and I will let you see your dream
and touch myself and think it's you

Have thanks princess divine, your eyes,
I've fallen deeper than I thought
I'll swipe twice more and would you please
reveal the beauty of your chest

Thank you, my strong and handsome suitor,
I took these shots for you,
my tiny hands are yours of course
how do they feel to you?

Saliva flooding in my mouth
my hands did squeeze and feel it all
such warmth and softness, each so cute
my tongue is longing for a taste

Have thanks for showing me your youth
for sending these with smiling eyes
I wonder, could I ask you to
… if you don't mind, you know…

But darling friend, just need to say
you know I will do anything
for you and only you I will
swipe it three times, amount the same

I do, I did, can't wait for it
what will you show me of yourself?
How can I go to bed and sleep
and miss the pictures coming in
I'll wait in feverish fire 'til
your message gets to me

Here it is now, I pause and wait,
before I click I brush my teeth, and hair,
wash face and hands and wipe the table clean
as if you come to me

My heart begins to pound, I click
and there your words in dreamlike scribe
'My darling handsome prince,' you write,
but you would know, you wrote it.

Have thanks to swipe your card three times
I sent you four so you may know
how much you mean to me
I'd do it all for free, you see,
if I had no need of money

The first you'll like, my skirt from school,
still fits me now, come have a peak,
the blouse too from a time long gone
in purest white, unbuttoned some

The next shows just how hot it is
the summer's heat just makes me boil
I had no choice, the blouse is off
please do not show it to your friends

I lift my skirt, what do you see?
Suspenders and black stockings,
you know the type, with buttons,
this close-up shows of what I mean

I roll each slowly down my leg,
they are so long now, you agree?
My toes still funny, as they were
since I was little girl of three
The last one shows, I'm lying down
exhausted from the heat

Oops, had to lift my skirt a bit
to let my bottom breathe
Princess of softest flesh, long hair,
your pictures make me stare
and care to draw you close,
I ache for scent of rose

But rose I only have but one
and once you've seen you'll leave,
alone I'll cry and you'll know why
for I shall miss you terribly

Three-hundred pictures, all of you
not one of all of you
a 100 bucks a pop I spent
and slowly getting broke

I know, dear darling, you've been good
with dream I woke this morn
that you sold house and all you have
and swipe to send to me
for you did promise that you would
give everything to me
I'm asking this of you to do
then you'll see all of me

but own none shall me while I live
that's all I need for me
but from the outside, all I am
I will show you to see

I did, dear princess, sold the house
and swipe I did, the lot
find thousands worth in your account
I ask, forget me not

A lot you asked, a lot you gave
now I shall keep my promise
darts of your generosity
have blown me to my knees
My shyness I shall face to bear
to honour what I said
I close my eyes so none can see
the inside of my soul

Dear friend, I know the ache you feel
and know what you've gone through
These shots, never reveal
to anyone but you

My mother, she would die of shame,
my father 'd kill me on the spot
Know this my friend, what you have done
has helped to feed so many

My parents do not know what bliss
they came to reap from swipes you did
and I shall never tell the truth
forever will deny it

Every piece of skin I own,
on any part of me
you now have pictures of it all
seen more of me than I can see

I hope you did enjoy the things
that you asked me to do,
that the result is as you'd hoped,
a dream that has come true

I do say thanks for all the swipes
it may seem high to you,
my youth only short-lived
as with each day

it goes 'til gone
that's all I have to bid

My fee will fall with each new fold,
some years from now none want to see
a girl that has grown old

And may I say what you don't know
your swipes does feed my family,
clothes my son and guarantees
he'll not be stupid girl as me

His path to university
for that I sell all that I can
to lift him from our poverty
this is my driving force, my friend

Perhaps the pictures that you have
can help sustain the bliss you ache
but if they don't, learn what I know
your heaven is a fantasy

It can drive you to anything
each picture as the breath you take
and after each you need one more
and never get enough

This curse some men don't know to flee
that's why I write these words,
think of a boy you helped to be
one day, provide for family
and think of that in memory
and you and I the only ones
know how it came to be

Know that your urge and thirsting did
in fact do good to us
that your good deed of swiping card
helped family with a new start

I am no easy girl, my friend,
had only one boy in my life
police one day came, took him in
he never did return
So judge me not for I must do
what any mother can,
with any means, use any tools
that I get in my hands

Video: https://youtu.be/NkjfxYMM_Zo

Like rats follow the piper (Trigger warning: Trauma)

I don't know what to say, I'm out of tears by now.
Each day is just a struggle, wished you were here back home.
Our baby is still drinking and grandma's leg is fine,
but the boy is missing you, alone he cries.

Three new chicks have hatched that I can write about.
The geese still on their nest, maybe next week we will know.
Things are going on here, things you need not know.
We've managed to survive, so far, tomorrow, who will know.

Men that have no foe fight strangers they don't know
and each would rather be in their own home.
Instead when they return, their legs left in the snow,
no arms to hold their children and their eyes no longer glow.

What does it mean to win, each side already lost.
Do those that give the orders know how much pain they cause.
Our son has lost his voice now, he'd seen too much to bear,
and when I set the table he stares at your empty chair.

The boy next door came back, in a box, the other day.
We've lined the street and paid respect and in silence we all prayed.
Don't come home in a box, dear, there are no flowers for a grave.
We've picked them all, the fields are bare and we could have used
some more.

The chicken thieves come as they please, even took the washing line.
The shops stripped bare, all plundered now, as they ship their loot
away.

The town you knew is gone and rubble fills the lanes,
the street-signs only hint of where things were before they came.

I know I can not send this, you will read between the lines.
My burden is not yours to bear, it's so heavy on my mind.
Each shot I hear I tremble, for it's another mother's son,
and she'll wail in pain and grieve for years not knowing why it's done.

So instead I write I miss you, ache to hold you in my arms.
We're all fine, please do not worry, don't come to any harm.
Guard the man that I married, he's the hero I adore.
Let no evil get inside you, with your light protect your core.

Rest in knowing that I love you, that I'm always at your side.
Shared embrace over far distance, stay safe my dear, survive.
We're on this earth a short while, on land we can never own,
the earth owns us, alive or dead, whichever flag is flown.

Is not the pain the same whatever side you're on?
What we had destroyed or plundered
and so many loved ones gone.
The so-called 'leaders' hide in mansions
play with lives they do not own,
and infect us with the evil seeds of the games they play alone.

And like rats follow the piper, but the piper's not in front,
always far from the living hell they cause, they never bear the brunt.
They are always well protected and their children safe and sound,
while their subjects wail in agony on blood-soaked foreign ground.

Video: https://youtu.be/-sUFfGe70tU

230226

death does not come with reason

all things must die, and so have I,
death does not come with reason
what did I do to live?
I hid behind the grains of sand
as snouts of boars gorged on my hatching siblings
at edge of dawn toiled through,
raced from the rising sun
thought safe, found crocs lay waiting still
cut short so many trails
dodged all to reach the cool,
escaped the birds, the fish, the sharks
that came to hunt, each made their claim,
I've travelled long, swam far and wide
each year our numbers thinning
but managed to grow old
no breath is left, as left I'm left
at sign that says 'Carcasses'
with arrow pointing right,
left next to remnants of a feast
all things must die, and so have I
as feast refused I boil amidst refuse,
on a garbage dump
death does not come with reason

Video: https://youtu.be/Xw34mBWBwaU

Hush (Trigger warning: Child abuse)

Hush, breathe no sound
the leaves are listening
the slightest breeze
will make them sway
and when they do
the forest knows
and all the leaves will whisper.

> How many challengers dared him?
> How many did he have to fight?
> How many came that sought me worthy as a prize?

Hush, breathe no sound.

> I need to know,
> the child I was is gone!

He fought not one,
none came to claim.

> And you stood by and let him take?

He's drunk, he doesn't know he did.

> I'm not, I do.
> Forever I shall carry this.
> I washed the sheets,
> so you not be upset

Knocked out I was,
another scar reminds.
Hush now,
this is your birthday.

> I am at five no more a child,
> What will I be at six, or ten?

Video: https://youtu.be/PACvDW0_uBI

A place away from town

We're going to save some money
for a place away from town
here we'll build a home
and settle down

on one side will be a forest
with trees 80 feet high
on the other side
a mountain touches the sky

We'll have space for 20 horses,
7 ducks, some geese, you'll see
2 big dogs, a cat
and you and me.

with a view towards the ocean
in the distance far away
and the nearest living soul
37 miles away

a creek twists through the meadows
wild flowers on each side
the buzz of dancing bees
and butterflies

bird songs before the sunrise
and slow rise of morning fog
birds greeting the sunrise
below the southern cross

approx 73, brisbane

Until forever

Painted a picture of your smile,
your golden hair and shining eyes
I have it hanging on the kitchen wall
you'll see, I think it's lovely

there is another on the other side
to keep your memories alive
yet you've been gone so many years ago
you're still alive inside me
every day, every night
every moment we're together

Our house has many walls you know
on each of them a painting goes
regardless of which way i turn around
i will find you all around me

and in each flower's bloom i see
your loving face that smiles at me
and should all petals take their leave, i'll know
you'll sleep

just for a short while
so you said years ago
and to this day you never left me

a treasured gift, memories
i hope they stay until forever
stay with me forever

Audio: https://soundcloud.com/heinz-ross/until-forever

Audio: https://heinzross.bandcamp.com/track/until-forever

(Music: 170122) (Lyrics: 31.01.2023)

Cease, to be (Trigger warning: Depression)

Jag-u-ar standing in thorns,
sharp-edged
broken
mirrors.

Cut paws, blood smudged,
puddles of tears.
Circles of perfection ripple,
drop joins pool.

Growl once, claw strikes,
ball of vision maimed.
Hiss, the last sound,
snow swallows Jag's echoes.

Jag-u-ar. Struck. Why?
Twin alone forever.

Cold set in, the place of fire
stoked with coal in summer.
Snow fell thick,
buried sound.

Summer heat, fire soaring
dried the last of twins.
Silence screams as snow fell thick
in season out of time.

Why? Jag-u-ar, why?
White speaks with lips
that have no sound.
Snow covers 'why' eight feet below.

Beneath, paws bleeding,
white coloured, no blue, none green,

twins needed to be seen,
sockets without purpose.

Summer sizzling, fires
roaring,
freezing cold
despite.

No day, no night,
twins gone,
feet on grass aware
that all is solid ice.

Sight void of vision,
sound screams in silent ache.
Smell of scentless snow.
Taste of tastelessness.

Touch numbed by shivering cold.
Steaming cold,
boiling frost.

Cease, to be.

19.10.2007

---

waif of vail

. unsaid
. word unread

Thought in . trance
. dance
. chance
speaking unspoken .

Beneath
. deepest depth . .
cliff's upper ridge reveals
below a cave, constrains the fading waive

As cold retains its answers, unthawed be
'til sigh may reach the voice contained, the key
that's trapped for aeons, thou shan't see,
bounce back to thee

Reversed, the small that bark on stilts
their bodies higher than the hills
no want of nearness to thy maker
risen above' the maker made

Another tower lied, the flight,
the climbing kite reached soaring high,
the mighty fell, the sleeping woken
from the fright

Weep spawned
waif dawned
whence is

Once cat that graced in daring leap the sight
that sought the calm found qualm,
offended by the alms
that ye present to feast

The wave of sound unwoven,
hurt,
too weak to weave again.

Thus, break thy must
for fail of need,
thyself is left of self,
one once, apart
too weak to seed,
too frail to breathe

Pained cry, as yon is nigh
the threads unwind the knit
as height's beneath the feet,
there, thou shall find thy it.

Once crown sat soaring loft,
thy crown a lie,
thy crown begins falling,
discerped thou find thyself.

Thy crown lies smashed,
thy ache for needing thrashed,
thy known all trashed,
thy line of life severed and slashed,
unfound the . still roving

Ye drips, the barren sand to soak
a stain of witness be that's left
of life that once fuelled cells of needing,
mutely gored

Uncloaked, oh precious dew,
unable to renew,
thyself to dwell in wordless realm
of ever calm

Sad silence galls
thou tall, once, falls
drained it stained
the ocean

Bondage,
vagabondage,
bond,
bonding
n age
n ageing,

Oh my,
enemy,
enema,
animosity
that thee . power hast to halt,
midst brave of failings,
wilt

Dare . awaken one in sleep
never to find the resting, once awoken
now, becoming just now,
then, then,
then once it was

Oh noble be,
thou jester, unborn blood of royalty,
a waif that's pained in history,
there, all the wanting, need of thee

30-10-2007 - 21-11-2007

Giants

Your future bleak in choosing
the spot I found you dwell
the white line separating
north and south bound
giants zooming
toward, and you held still
and there you learned
that if you do, they'd go away.

No space to run, no place to go
no hiding spot remained, no room for fear
as fast approaching giants near.
Shut eyes help in pretending that they're not;
each coming closer to your spot.
What can you do, but think of calmer days

This place of dwell, a hell with roaring
winds to cut your eyes, and so did I
not knowing you'd be there.

Canadian tune Canadians know, was humming
in my ear, as I approached as giant to get
near you, and sensed the trap you're in.

Oh precious life of colour bright
no giant knows you're there.
The giants kill, not knowing that you ever were.
And as I turned to double check, confirmed
my eye was right in spotting you
and was I glad, to find you, you were still alive.

A newborn maple leaf to grow, near lake
with name of Huron,
to shelter, giving rest.

07-11-2008

Drops of Dew

Thy chalice fills with drops of dew,
thy ache thou born to be
to join the paining remnants that
the suffer caused to thee.

No feast to feast, no sip to quench
and with the softest cloth of satin
wipe the forehead's drops excreting
purity of pain.

Thou feet in mud, the head in clouds,
both failing sight to see
thou sword has lost its blade,
but lost thou has not yet
thou shield.

Eye tries to lie, to un-see seen,
but saw it did and spit will cover much too late.
Unread read, un-hear said, undo done,
fail to succeed.

Else un-know known,
ignore.

04-11-2007

Dew

Sad-eyed gold-haired princess smiled
at seed she found by chance,
slipped from her hand, fell to the ground,
unaware of this she danced.

Wind buried seed, snow covers soil
frozen it lay in wait
in the bitter cold the spring arrives
the sun refused the ice to thaw.

Another season void of snow,
the sun so hot it baked the ground.
Moisture flees by rising up
to wilt all that did dare to grow.

Third season came the dormant seed
awaits the light and drops of dew
that may give hope of growth and life
it knows within are due.

Three things a seed will need
or else will fail becoming proud,
a need of water, air and warmth
is all it asks of thee.

And ask it did for moisture,
for air and warmth from you
and in return it promised
to give the same to you.

A fair skinned maiden breaks the soil
a narrow gap to veil below.
The sunlight reached the resting seed
as signal starting growth.

The maiden's eye shed tear of pain,
which fell into the crack.
The dew of hope absorbed,
the torpid seed awakes.

The maiden drains her well of dew
while the seed is germinating,
embryonic tissues grow,
transform the germ to seedling.

Last drop of dew she parted,
which turned from pain to joy,
as the seedling sent its roots
to depth and width to help it grow.

And then it held onto the soil
its fragile head uncoiled,
in reach towards her warmth, its sun
that the maiden's heart sent out.

Its root reached deep and spread across
underneath the ground,
holding it fast in any wind,
to grow in strength and girth.

And as it reached maturity
the once seed said to thee,
'thank you for the dews of hope
that once you gave to me.'

Now I have grown to what my seed knew
that I had to be
and in your eye's reflection
I see I am a tree.

Once I made a promise
to give the same to you
and on each leaf each morning
I'll give a drop of dew.

And in each fruit I'm growing
a feast to quench your thirst,
and in each branch I shed,
enough to give you warmth.

And in the night I shall inhale
the gas you cannot breathe,
and in return give oxygen
so clean that it will please.

And loft it grew a canopy
as cover from the rain and sun.
Its trunk and branches thickened
to be a home for one.

And when it reached its glory
dressed in blossoms' bloom,
its scents to reach all bees, and birds
sang songs of joy and doom.

And countless fruits it grew in time
all fell with seeds of hope,
and lovers came to carve their names
on its trunk for all to see.

cvs, 19 - 24-June-2008

The Road

Life's up and down, a constant change
sometimes life seems to dwell;
Mirage to disappear before
it could be held.

Coyote wails in cold of night
its head stretched to the moon
that casts its shadow underneath,
as if it were a hole of doom.

However long a night might be
the sun will dart its rays
and chase it to the other side,
transforms the night to day.

An hour spent without your voice
seems as a day without a sound,
a day without a sign of you
is as a week of night.

A week without the shining lights
your eyes beam from your face to mine,
I can't imagine how long that
would feel to be.

In days without you sunshine scores
to boil the ocean off the shores
to rise as vapour growing high
to build a castle in the sky.

A dreamlike castle floats in air
with golden glow as frame, he stares.
But in the clouds no eagle rests,
no stick to be as porch, no nests.

All it can be is rain at best
only the joker knows the jest.
The sun's rays render hopers blind
reflecting surface waters, sigh.

The cloud of dreams distorted
by ripples on the waters.

Despite the branch across the path,
the screech of bird, shell in the sand,
the need to head towards
is greater than a cautious stand.

'How do I find my home,' he asks,
'Describe your home?' she questions,
and when he did she knew it was
the same place she was seeking.

Then she set out and so did he
to seek the home they'd never seen,
and forth they went in hopeful bliss
until the road forked in the mist.

And if the words come to a halt
I shall have failed in trying all,
it's then the magpie sings the call,
'Have faith, don't fear, the sun is near.'

It lifts the heavy haze from view,
she's seen to walk the highway,
the other on a dirt road where the
rocks had fallen, trees decayed and
stones and boulders blocked his way.

He climbed across to follow
where the road once must have been
to find it all had washed away
and further on had overgrown with weeds.

For three more days she moved ahead,
and wondered where the highway lead,
'til in the curve it came to end
and turned to grass and sand.

A new dusk came that turned to night,
uncertain both edged through the dark,
an owl showed one above the light,
a distant star as mark.

A new dawn breaks and she looks 'round
the land in morning sun,
so peaceful and serene, yet so alone
if one is one. It doesn't feel like home.

A falcon soars to mountain ridge,
while he stood at the forest's edge,
this view so rich if he could share
with one that feels so near.

He took a tree's shadow as sign
walking cross country in straight line.
She saw a twinkle in the east
and tracked a flock of flying geese.

And in the afternoon that day,
she stopped, in silent voice to say,
'This does feel different, it feels good,
It seems as if I'm being wooed.'

The orange ball of sun did set
and in its glare his silhouette.
'I feel a calm and harmony,
maybe because of you,' said she.

The fading sun blinding her eye
she could not see who did approach,
but when she recognised his face
she saw that it was he. She sighed.

She said, 'Oh, it is you, my friend.'
'Sorry to disappoint,' said he,
'we walked a different path,
despite, we met again.'

'To meet you in this golden light
brings pleasure to my heart,' said he,
'but if you were to close your eyes
perhaps you'll see inside my shell.'

'Home is not here, home is not there,
but with you home is everywhere,
as long as I am near your glow
my heart is calm, it knows.'

But often eyes will render blind
if one compares a dream and sight
and eyes can never seem to find
the jewels of the soul.

cvs 24-27 Jun 2008

sign here

      sign here
what am I signing for?
      6 degrees
who sent it
      it is your command of 6 months ago
is it 6 degrees plus or minus?
      plus
It's already 39 degrees C
      please sign, thank you
      it's now 45 C, order delivered
what's the point of that?
      you've asked for it
in winter I did

      sign here
Jessie? where is she?
      after you sign, thank you
      go ahead, you will meet her
      in a few minutes, bye
are you Jessie?
      yes, I am
gee, wow, but I thought you were a girl
      that I am
you're all grown up
      so, don't you like me?
I do, very much so, but...
      am I not as you wished?
much more than I could have...
      then you will find it easy to fall in love with me
but I am already in love
      oh, that was quick, but thank you
someone else I meant
      that is wonderful, did you need more?
      was she not enough or why did you...

I did before I met her
       I was your wish, I am your wish fulfilled
yes
I also wished for a child, a daughter, I thought you'd…
       I am not your daughter
yes, I know, who will be her mother?
       you will decide, she needs to be born
       she's not yet conceived
       sign here
what is it this time?
       you don't want to know
not now, please…
       sorry, it's my job
what if I don't sign?

© Heinz Ross, Gold Coast, Australia, 10 Nov 2008

Water

A pebble,
however small, thrown into a pond
will generate ripples in all directions.
That is the nature of water.

It can also rise above,
become vapour, renew countless times
and even freeze to a solid,
change its name to ice.

We are of water.

7 Jan 2008

---

dead bird's feathers

once both shared this feeling
of love and to belong
brought happiness,
nothing seemed wrong

both were certain
that this love would not fail
both thought that love would be
the calm in any gale

why did it break apart?
out come all the reasons
one can't absorb the words
for all have a solution

yet one did love the other,
still does
that much they knew
now as if they had never known
the closeness that they had, is there
in memory for the aching

love is a seed, so fragile,
needing due care to grow
that much they knew
sill failed it, unaware,
that it took flight and left.
Who is to blame?

A pillow is just a bag
filled with dead bird's feathers

27 Jun 2008

Lorraine's gifts (Trigger warning: Suicide)

At 8 she was a pretty girl
slight wave in her black hair
her voice clear as a nightingale
her songs to fill the air

And in the night she dressed in white
and walked along the sand
the moon above reflecting on the waves

that crashed on land

At 12 she drew in colours
and shapes of wondrous kind
so intricate and faint, soft shades
to bring her art to life

And in the night she dressed in white
and walked along the sand
the moon did cast her shadow
coloured as her thoughts inside

At 18 she did use her hands
to give the moist clay shape
and when it dried, each one sighed
her sculpture spoke in dimmest light

And in the night she dressed in white
and walked along the sand
thoughts of darkness choked her throat
a jar of pills she held

At 22 her depth of thought
expressed in poetry
that reached the hearts of everyone
stirred souls that could not feel

And in the night she dressed in white
and walked along the sand
her eyes did stare, her right hand bare,
her left hand held a blade

At 26 this special girl
adored by all she met
acclaim and recognition brought
much honour and respect

And in the night she dressed in white
and walked along the sand
at ebb she sat, began to cry
until she changed the tide

At 30 she no longer sang,
no longer wrote or mixed the paint
each work cost her a piece of life
she'd never find again

And in the night she dressed in white
and walked along the sand
to wonder, all the gifts of joy
left her depressed and waned

At 34 she thought to trade her gifts
for peace of mind
fertilisers took her voice
her hand and arm a fall had mauled

And in the night she dressed in white
and walked along the sand
the moon above reflecting on the waves
she didn't care

At 38 her torment grew
her insides drained and bare
she'd hide her sadness with a smile
no love of life left in her eye

And in the night she dressed in white
and walked along the sand
her body weak, her strength all spent
her thoughts consumed by 'end'

At 42 she thought she knew
and this set out to do
all the gifts one once could see
brought agony and misery

And on that night she dressed in black
and walked along the sand
took pills and poison, slid her wrist
and life ran from her vein

The trail of blood soaked in the sand
toward the rip she swam
the next wave cleared her traces
as if she'd never been

But now before the day turns night
the sinking sun is red
it's shine reflecting on the waves
ever since she's dead

29.June-7.July.2008

Princess Alyd

The King rode out one morning
to where he'd never been
and in the distance spied a girl
that never he had seen.

Upon her shoulder resting,
a sharp-eyed bird of prey,
it opened wings and flew from her
towards the King, a screech she heard.

He sent his horse to seek her
as he stood back to see.
The girl turned 'round, towards the sound
and wondered what it'd be.

The falcon loft and gliding
towards the horse it flew,
to land upon the stallion's back
and called to her, she knew.

'Who have you brought to meet me?'
she'd ask the bird of prey,
the horse exhales through nostrils
to snort the air away.

The horse approached her closer,
her hands reached for his mane,
'Maybe your rider's injured,
a knight perhaps or thane?'

The horse lay down beside her
and head to head they'd rest,
the bird of prey then flew away,
his screech heard from the west.

The King could not believe
to what his eyes had seen,
the wildest stallion in the land
resting beside a teen.

Towards he walked.
'Who's there?' she called.
'It's I,' said he and so said she,
'We both can't be the same.'

'Do you not recognise me?'
the King did say to her.
'Kind sir, forgive me that I don't,
my eyes are in the bird.'

'Then you would have the sharpest eyes,
that I have ever seen.'
'Maybe that's so, but I don't know.
No longer can I see.'

'Are you a nobleman or thief?'
this she did ask of him.
'I am no thief or nobleman,
a poor old beggar, this I am.'

'But in your voice you seem to me
not beggar I could sense,'
'But if it is the truth, you say,
know each day brings a chance.'

'Who knows, each day may be a gift
in which you find your treasures
if this is what you're seeking,
or else may bring you pleasures.'

'This morning I set out to ride,
I had no wish at all,
except the Babel in my head would stop
this is my only ail.'

'Do tell me, what's your name and why,
the falcon has your eye?'
'I do have eyes inside my head,
but lost my sight, I'm blind.'

'I come from far away, kind sir,
in the east they know my name
as Princess Alyd of high birth
but so much has since changed.'

'Three years ago, my parents,
King and Queen of the land,
arranged for me to meet a Prince
to be his bride one day.'

'I was fourteen and much too young,
and this the Prince could see,
I found him bed another,
not wait his time for me.'

'After I cried and tears I dried,
darkness came in the day to stay,
and ever since it happened
has never gone away.'

'I left all gold and treasures,
forfeit claim of my crown and ran,
and left the kingdom far behind
to never hear his voice again.'

'The falcon has been with me
since I was a small child,
has always warned of dangers,
he's like a guarding shield.'

'So sad to hear your story,
the Prince a fool, unworthy,
of such sweet jewel as you are,
understandable antipathy.'

'If it was I, I'd wait for you,
most special Princess Alyd,
I'd wait three-hundred years or more
for the chance that I could marry.'

'You at my side, you as my bride,
would please this heart of mine,
but I'm just a poor, old beggar man
picking grapes along the Rhine.'

'I may not have the gift of sight,
each sunny day for me is night,
but all my senses say I'm right,
that you're no beggar man.'

'In all my life, never did see
a beggar on a stallion,
a healthy horse, well groomed and clean
unless of course, it's stolen.'

'But as you said, you're not a thief
this I can feel is true,
you as beggar, I shan't believe
better think of something new.'

'Kind sir, may I do use my hands
to feel your skin and face,
as they can show me parts of you,
unless this makes you fazed.'

'Please do,' said he, and she reached out
her fingertip to rest
between his eyebrows it remained,
said she, 'No beggars clothes you vest.'

'Be still,' she said, 'your Babel's gone,
I cannot sense it here.'
'You're right,' said he, 'it left me,
when I saw you standing there.'

'That's good,' she said, 'it will not come
to bother you again,
your head is free to cast a wish
that shall come true today.'

And then she cupped her hands
around his face to feel it's shape,
and pleased she smiled and said to him,
'No beggar stands as scape.'

He grinned at her perception
and asked her, 'Would you be,
the Queen of just a beggar man
or whom you find in me?'

'Kind sir,' she said, 'your wish granted
before I heard your voice,
your stallion told me of your need,
the falcon screeched it's choice.'

Says she, 'would it not be a burden,
to wed a girl that's blind?'
'You see more with your fingertips
then I see with my eyes.'

The King did lift the Princess
upon the stallion's back
and returned to his castle
to announce their day of wed.

In white long gown with trailing train
she walked towards the King,
and in his hand he held a crown
and said to her, 'My Queen.'

And colourful reflections
danced on her face that day
from stained glass mosaic art works
and the jewels in the crown.

A band of gold, he slid to wear
for her as wedding ring
before her eye's the night took flight
she saw his face and said to him:
'My King.'

cvs 29 Jun.2008

Once in a Lifetime Sale

The Supermarket's sign announced
'Once in a Lifetime Sale.'
'Doors open 6am until
they shut tonight at eight.'

Anger went, 5 cents a pound
until anger sold out.
Fear on sale, aisle 17
neatly wrapped, new, nice and clean.

Shelf underneath has packs of shame,
nine for the price of six,
the same for sticks of hatred,
sadness and regrets.

Rage deep inside the freezer box
together with aggression,
horror diced in bags of four,
buy six and suffering is free.

Paranoia, worry, terror,
just a coin per pound.
At half price is hostility
1/3 off panic, guilt and grief.

'Excuse me, but where could I find,'
a young man asks: 'some empathy,
forgiveness and compassion?'
The staff swallows surprise and chews regret.

Pride sliced in strips, sold by the foot,
just as doubt, envy and humiliation,
last chance to stock your shelves at home,
apathy, pain and agitation.

Old lady wants to barter all her suffering of late
for calmness and some happiness
and trade her sorrow for some joy
instead annoyance filled the shelves.

A man in uniform came in
to look for courage, confidence
and righteous indignation,
but found surprise, ambivalence,
his trolley loaded to the brim
with boxes of disappointments.

Mum with three kids searching the aisles
for privacy, security.
'Is this for me?' her eldest asks,
'Oh no, this is for me,' said she.

'I'll get you caution and surprise,'
and for the youngest one she picked
some gratitude and pleasure.
But calmness is for number two,
before he kicks his brother.

The information desk responds
to answer questions, offer help.
Two items most did ask to find
but none could find it in the shelves.

'Where then is love and where is hope?'
'They sell that further down the road,
as we no longer stock these items.
The refunds send us almost broke.'

'But why do you sell most of this so cheap?'
one buyer asks the manageress.
'It is a Sale, that's what Sales do,
we guarantee the lowest price to you.'

'But who would want to pay a coin,
for three bags of depression?'
'You'd be surprised, Sir, many do,
as you can see we're almost out.'

'The shelves of cowardice and greed
are empty, see them bare,
as well as hatred, cruelty and fear,
there must have been a need
and all the stress is gone as well.'

'Your pricing is to blame,' said he.
'Unhappiness is 4 cents for a box of nine,
while 60 coins will buy the opposite, per box of three.'
'I see,' said she, 'demand, availability dictate the price.'
'You sell no hope but sell despair
that is not fair,' said he.
'You'll find frustration in the last aisle, Sir,'
He said, 'It seems I get enough for free.'

'Perhaps you need anxiety and we will add some apathy
a dozen sticks euphoria and a little bit of ecstasy,
all in all just 5 cents for the lot,
a bargain basement price, would you agree or not?'

'Even if you paid me for the goods
I don't think I'll be tempted.'
'But Sir, we have a gift-wrap service,
what you can't use, give to your friends.'

He laughed and searched the exit of the store.
'For less get more, we buy in bulk
and we have stores around the world,'
she called, as he walks through the door.

8.July 2008

Decoding the Satirical Supermarket: A Commentary on 'Once in a Lifetime Sale'

The poem "Once in a Lifetime Sale" presents a satirical take on the commodification of human emotions in a supermarket setting. In this cleverly crafted piece, the poet delves into the absurdity of attempting to package and sell complex feelings as if they were tangible products.

The poem invites readers to step into a unique supermarket where emotions line the shelves, neatly wrapped and priced for purchase. From anger sold by the pound to neatly packaged fear in aisle 17, the poet creatively portrays a world where feelings are transactional commodities.

The use of a 'Once in a Lifetime Sale' sign introduces a layer of irony, as the mundane act of purchasing emotions clashes with the implied rarity of such an opportunity. This contradiction prompts reflection on the inherent contradiction of attempting to commercialize deeply personal and ephemeral experiences.

The interactions between customers and staff within the poem offer a humorous commentary on the futile pursuit of positive emotions. The search for empathy, forgiveness, and compassion meets with unexpected responses, shedding light on the scarcity of these desired sentiments in the market.

The poem cleverly parodies traditional sales tactics, with the manageress explaining the pricing strategy based on demand and availability. The almost sold-out status of certain negative emotions humorously underscores the prevalence of such feelings in society.

References to stores around the world and buying in bulk hint at the global nature of the societal trends under scrutiny. The dark humour in suggesting the gift-wrapping of unwanted emotions for friends adds a final ironic touch to the commentary, highlighting the absurdity of treating emotions as tradable commodities.

At its core, 'Once in a Lifetime Sale' serves as a poignant social commentary on the contemporary inclination to reduce profound human experiences to marketable products. The poem prompts readers to reflect on the societal emphasis on negativity and the challenges of finding positive emotions in a world seemingly obsessed with commodification.

In conclusion, this thought-provoking piece offers a unique lens through which to examine the intersection of consumerism and the deeply personal realm of human emotions. The juxtaposition of the mundane act of shopping with the profound nature of feelings prompts readers to question the societal priorities reflected in this satirical supermarket.

Ayo (Trigger warning: Rape, Loss)

The child was born late afternoon
his mother never heard him cry,
she passed out giving birth to him
and never made a sigh.

'May you find realm of peace,'
said she, the grandma of the boy
and closed his mother's eyes to cease,
for she won't need them anymore.

'Your mother gave you life,' she said,
'her life was hard, my boy.'
'Despite her misery and pain,
I shall name you joy.'

'Ayo, my boy, that is your name,
you may not travel far,
you will die long before your time,
your light the faintest of all stars.'

'You'll want to know about your pa
might as well tell you now,
you will not have the time to wait
to ask me when you've grown.'

'I don't know who your father is,
nor did your mother know,
so many took her body,
as others did before.'

'They all came running, crossed the fields
and waved their long blades in the air
and caused us fear, we ran away
but when you're ill the legs give way.'

'When she was young, your mother, dear,
she fetched the water from the creek
eight other girls did go with her
and only four returned in tears.'

'All under 12, the girls had been,
men's hate and lust they'd never seen,
but from that day we learned to dig
the graves for our children.'

'You'll ask, where were the men to help,
to keep us safe from harm,
we buried most and some we nursed,
deep cuts, lost hands and arms.'

'Our homes in flames, they pushed us out
to wander through the land,
always in fear of being seen
spent time in hiding from the men.'

'And then the sickness grew within
infections of the men girls carried
and all the children they did bear
we have already buried.'

'Ayo, my boy, and so in you
born without chance to grow,
the sickness that's inside of you
will give you no defence at all'

'And you'll ask why, I wish I knew,
a woman's door cannot be locked,
the beasts that came did never ask,
forced entry without knocking.'

'And those that tried to keep them out
were beaten, kicked and slaughtered,
and left for dead where they were found,
those girls were our daughters.'

'We lost or homes, we lost our place
and with it our identity.'
'I do not know where we are now
or how we'll manage to survive.'

'We live life worse than animals
and try to find some things to eat,
we hide from those with hateful eyes
and are in fear of all we meet.'

'So in this first hour of your life
you know the suffering of your tribe,
for we're not strong and far dispersed
and dwindle by the day.'

'I'd rather face the wildcats, lions,
than all the beasts called men,
for they kill swiftly with their jaws
and save us lots of pain.'

'This cradle of humanity,
birthplace for all the world did see,
will not grant life for poor and weak
and starving orphans that are sick.'

'Ayo, this day you're born to be,
heard all the things I said,
I'll hold you close, a moment's joy
may all we ever get.'

10-11.July 2008

Echoes of Suffering: Ayo's Tale

This poignant poem, titled "Ayo," delves into the harsh realities of life through the lens of a grandmother addressing her newborn grandson. The poem addresses themes of loss, suffering, and the impact of violence on a community.

The narrative begins with the description of the child's birth, a moment that should bring joy and hope. However, the tone is immediately sombre as it's revealed that the mother never heard her child cry, having passed out during childbirth. The grandmother takes on the role of both narrator and caregiver, offering a grim perspective on the world into which the child, Ayo, is born.

The grandmother's words paint a stark picture of the hardships endured by the community. The mother's tragic circumstances during childbirth, symbolizing vulnerability and powerlessness, set the stage for a narrative of pain and sorrow. The grandmother's act of closing the mother's eyes signifies an end to her suffering, but it also underlines the harsh reality that she won't need her eyes in the afterlife.

Ayo's naming becomes a poignant moment in the poem, as the grandmother chooses to name him "joy" despite the misery and pain surrounding his mother's life. This contrasts sharply with the foretelling of Ayo's short life, described as "you will die long before your time, your light the faintest of all stars." This anticipation of an early death reflects the grim fate awaiting him.

The poem sheds some light on the grim circumstances surrounding the mother's life and the broader community. It touches upon the violence faced by the women, the loss of children, and the brutality of the men who caused such suffering. The imagery of the girls fetching water and the subsequent tragedy that unfolds highlights the vulnerability of women and children in the face of violence.

The grandmother's lamentation expands to encompass the loss of homes, identity, and the degradation of the community. The description of living worse than animals, hiding from those with hateful eyes, and the overall atmosphere of fear paints a bleak picture of the survival struggles faced by this community.

The closing lines emphasize the harsh reality of the world, comparing the brutality of men to wild animals. The grandmother expresses a preference for facing natural predators over the dangers posed by fellow humans. The concluding stanzas touch on the broader social issues, criticizing a world that denies life to the poor, weak, and sick.

In its entirety, "Ayo" serves as a powerful commentary on societal injustice, violence against women, and the profound impact of a harsh environment on the most vulnerable members of a community. The poem prompts reflection on the human condition, the cycles of suffering, and the urgent need for empathy and change.

My Universe

My Universe, a silvery sphere, inside
surfaced with triangular reflecting plates
that are arranged all around itself
to form the outer space of shell.

Self-centred shines the brightest jewel
with name of 'I' to form the core.
Within I an eye that can see
in all directions all at once.
All it can see when looking outwards
is self from all its bounced reflections.

This universe provides no shades
as all its focus is the core,
and as the jewel burns in brightness
the focal point will heat it more.

Fuelled by the self-inflicting pain
the core's heat rises manifold,
to raise the temperature of mirrors
that makes the sphere shine in a glow.
Incessantly this unique jewel
burns within and multiplied
the heat begins to consume I.

Close to the point of self-destruction
the bonds that hold the plates transform,
melt from the propagating heat-waves
that bombard it ever more.

The bond that fails allows the plate
to detach from its neighbours,
and one by one each joint that lets go
embarks to change my universe.

A sphere with many cracks it seems
launches it to grow in size,
exploding outwards from the jewel
to help it cool, to save its life.

The eye of I, now for the first time
can see further than itself,
it is in awe of what it finds
and ever more so
as it's shell grows
and expands,
freed to be blind.

And there another silvery sphere
glows in perilous light,
the star of 'you' it traps within
until it too can melt its chains.

I'm not alone at all, I find,
another there beside me,
I hope to see you in your light,
your emanating glory.

And just beyond, illumination,
another you and you and more,
and there's a 'he', a 'she', an 'it',
a 'we', an 'us', a 'those' and 'these',
and 'them' as well to see.

Yet each unique as I, a jewel,
and from their own core
each is I, yet often see the other,
as if they are not there at all.

But there is where I once was too
perhaps still am, what do I know,
what lens distorts my vision
that I am yet to find.

But can I say, you're beautiful,
a star with brightest light,
magnificent and rare to find
yet by the billions, seen to shine.

So let my eye thank you to see,
the splendour of your being,
the treasured gift of showing me
allowing me the feast in seeing.

However bright your star may shine
behind it trails a cone of shade
from each of all the other lights
that surround your outer self.

The parts that formed my sphere
expanding, triangular plates,
reflecting gleam,
so distant now, so small to see
blending as debris in the seen
in time to perish out of sight.

Yet once they formed a light tight sphere,
a shell, within as burning hell,
as outer edge
and all it could
is focus on the core.
Not anymore, my universe
has blown to bits,
and so it be,
and so be it.

12.July.2008

voice of want

oh still be now, you voice of want
deceive me with your calling
awaken thirst and hunger
to tell me that you're need

how often did I fall for you
each time my knees were bleeding
how often did my hands reach out
to be just short of reach

oh still be now, you low amp thought
just one transmitter rang your bell
before you grow much further
and turn my life to hell

may neurons find a detour
to starve this want of life
before you start infecting me
and all my body strikes

tease you may and tempt you do
and like gunpowder flaming
the tiniest ignition would take
years of tiring taming

let go, I ask, leave me alone
your falsehood I discovered
you are but wishful thought
that tries to impregnate reality

want is want and need is need
a clear line of distinction
yet you declare your eminence
in paramount importance

dilating grand delusions
sold as real and true to me
like climbing weed that strangles tree
none reach the sky but you

the tree will die from parasite
but you proclaim you're paradise
indoctrinating feel-good thought
is all you'll ever be to me

a parasite you are
that feeds off all my being
deep reaching brainwash powder that
with each hit is growing louder

I do not wish to hear the voice
of want and begging claim
as single minded desperation
will it invade my brain

be still then, hear the golden voice
of silence without sound
yet smell the music of the clouds
and see the colours of the night

and feel a thought of textured glass
before it came to be
billions of sand grains tease the sense
taste what you know you hear and see

13.July 2008

Tomorrow

Tomorrow is the day
when you will cease your wailing
when you will stop your calling
your dawn display of restlessness
that echoes from the lake
before the first sounds of the birds
that you awake each day

Tomorrow is the day
when all your calls be answered
the last days of July enough
to bring forth August
time so special
feared that you could not oblige
each of your fibres' yearning

How often did I smile
at your persistence?
Each day your eyes did scan the sky
and then you'd dive
and splash the waters

groom to perfection
all your beauty
and look again at far horizon,
so many there, but none
for you.

The rising sun,
brilliant display of sparkling waters
amongst the lilies and the reeds
bathing your shape in splendour,
drying warmth to tease the droplets off
so they return where they belong.

Your folds prepared for weeks,
now is the time to make a home.
I know the urgency your calls proclaim to one and all.

Just one more night,
I promise
you'll call just one more time,
as night begins to hide
and I shall sleep 'til 10
but then awake, I'll drive away

when I return
you'll come greet me
as you do,

rewarded find your wishes
your tireless hope,
your ache and need of mothering
given another chance.

And may you find the one I bring
reflect the vision of your needing

blue eyed gander, quacking echoes
craving sight of your desire,

may you mate until you're tired,
grow six eggs and build a nest
sit for weeks in brooding pose
to incubate your offspring
while you both be guarding
them from all and any
that may wish them harm.

And now you live your dream.

And sit you did, for weeks in silent pose
each day a noisy dash to fly,
land in the dam, to gulp
in hurried haste and then return
to place your moist down
'round your eggs, to radiate
your warmth and incubate
the coming lives

September 10th, the day they hatched
seven yellow fluffy goslings followed you
onto the grass
and blue-eyed gander hissing
to any non geese coming near them

I found one more lay in the nest,
the egg with crack revealed another,
half the beak was out,
its head still curved into its body

and in high squeaks it called for help
to get it out of the hard shell

And when you heard the call you
came, all family behind you,
one look and then you sat,
your offspring gathered close,
hiding under the safety of your wings

It finally came true,
your dream of motherhood rewarded,
the many years of trying past,
the many months of fruitless brooding,
it happened once and gave you eight

So many eyes join in your joy
but be aware, not all are kind,
the foxes are gone
but high up reigns the falcon,
he can stand silent in the sky,
his eyes are sharp and he is swift

The slow approaching snakes
would love to get a little closer,
they are not always slow,
especially with the weather warming
But have no fear,
you now have twenty eyes.

15 Jul -10 Sep.2008

---

rain drops

I hope the rain drops hummed a tune
of ease and inner calm,
of time that heals, of time that grows
your hope that tells of shine

I hope they soothed you off to sleep
and calmed you not to cry
I hope the heavens cried for you
and took away your sigh

I hope the morning light may touch
your eyes with golden glow
and with it a new day begins
that helps your dream to grow

3-June-2008

Mother of two

Imagine, you're a mother,
your daughter's grown,
same size as you, despite
she's just a baby.

She follows you,
watches what you do,
she screams for food,
you feed her.
No matter what you find,
it's not enough,
she screams for more.

Every step you take,
she's in your ear,
'food, food',
and you run off your feet to find it.

You show her how to pick it up
and shove it down her gob.
She gulps it down;
she starts anew,
'food, food.'

But worst of all,
it's not just her,
she also has a sister,
who shadows every move you do,
she too calls out for more.
I feel for you,
mother of two,
especially if they're Magpies.

18.Oct 2008

Perhaps

we are born to live
we live to die
and while we're living
we are dying
as long as we're alive
we cannot be dead
we only live
whilst we're not dead
but once we're dead
we're not alive
except in thoughts
and in the bits
we leave behind,
which then transform
to live again
with parts of us within
therein the magic that links all
those that have been,
those yet unborn,
as plant or living thing we change
in endlessly becoming
so at this time, I do contain
parts of my foe from long ago
and parts of many I don't know
and so does he or she
comprise parts of my ancestry
why do we spent energy to hold
a grudge for centuries or more
and close our eyes and ears and minds
instead of letting go
in each we come to meet in life
we face our mirror, rearranged,
sometimes believe it is another
when all along each is a brother,
sister, mother

while we're busy speaking
we cannot hear the silence
while the eye mostly absorbs
it also transmits good and bad
despite a 20/20 vision
I prove my blindness every day
I look elsewhere, perhaps forget
and hope the seen will go away
we come, and whilst we're coming
we also go away
I cannot be here and then claim
to be there at once as well
but could be anywhere at all
once at a time
my heart is pushing blood
and sucks,
a muscle pulls
but cannot push
a cold heart may need
a hot hatred
or something else as fuel
we give
we take
we know so much
and know so little of everything
we criticise and we admire
and our hunger rarely tires
we love
we hate
we can give love
we cannot take it from,
and while I think of you
I cannot think of her or him,
these or those or anyone
but where is love that
never had a chance to grow
what did one grow instead ,

what if what's missing
one had never had
and where is tolerance, restraint,
understanding and regret,
unbalanced by our greed and creed
and powerless defeat
while some thought we had won
some lid the kindling that did light
flicker of motivation
the winds of time will fan the flame
imbued with righteous indignation
out of control inferno burns
peace loving guy becomes assassin
one could not hurt a fly but kill
we can our siblings, in the believe
of progress, regressing to another time
and what seems proper may contain
within the seed of being wrong
the ones we think to love today
we can turn hating, given pain
as I demand,
I'm doomed to fail
as I insist on being right
a dormant wrong will be my ail
do-gooders are so many
but those that do good far between
I am intelligent and stupid
this I can do, that I cannot
perhaps I could, if I just tried
but do I feel like it or not
within are all the contradictions
known to him and her and me
and as my thoughts colours my vision
I see just what I want to see
why would the brain attack the brain
we always have, when we're confused,
if not our own then that of our kind,
to me it is the same

why do we do what we do do
perhaps because we can
or become trapped in inner spaces
that are as a glass, filled to the brim
or full of emptiness

10.July 2008

---

deception

Nothing could be so deceiving.
as the righteous inner feeling
Fuelled by powerful conviction,
leaves no room left for doubt.

undisputed declaration that proclaims
That one is 'right.
when the spot grants no vision

grows beyond, consumes all sight,

disregards minute suspicions,

with unworthiness of thought

28. Jan 2010, Bam

---

hemimetamorphosis (Trigger warning: Depression)

oh, still be now
refrain from panting,
intimidate with staring eye
so that there are none
that may be sensing
the weak it needs to hide

frangible core
of living breast
that needs to guard
from whipping sound,
the anguish caused

by all their laughter,
even their silence pains

featherless wings,
frail powdered beauty
in fluttering flight,
erratic dance
as if to dodge
the tracing bullets,
intrepid in withdrawal
slowly to fade from sight,
despite,
dressed in adorning grace

sometimes they fail
to notice
depth
of hurt they cause
they lash out,
defend, attack, get even,
respond with
curt reply

not all, some freeze,
some die inside,
some hide
too tongue-tight to reply

darts from their eyes
injure and maim,
the eyes that stare away
still find their target,
pains no less

what is their pleasure
that they shatter
one inside,
so fragile, yet,

none there
to grasp the consequence
all could, none does

oblivious of blows
that reach
one deep within
and then they laugh,
'what's wrong', they say
and cannot comprehend

though none to see the missiles
that shot just once
seem to repeat,
like an incessant barrage
countless times,
each leave their marks,
so many
that one is left at sunrise
on a darkling path

one hides away,
repairs the coat,
the powder will not stick,
holes in the wings
right near the camouflaging eye
for all to look right through it
with no silk retreat
cocoon

20-24 July 2008

An object fell

If letter 'o' falls on a line
with high velocity,
it marks it with a dent
the shape of letter 'u'.

The line won't be the same
and letter 'o'
changed to curved 'underscore'.

Instead of letters, take a sphere,
6 feet across
that comes from there
or anywhere,
with speed just slower than the sound
and hits soft part of ground.

The hole it leaves 20 feet deep,
the soil compressed, sides very steep,
vertical drop,
as dent called a depression.

14.Oct.2008

---

inner universe

inside is as the outside
distance inverted
short space counts,

yet size of little relevance
as all the planets change around
depending on their closeness
to the sun, your core

once one is close
it blocks the view to others
becomes consuming,
overpowers all

arrhythmic cycles
some planets seem to stop,
park in their tracks
then they move on
next day or in two months from now

they're back
sometimes they stay away for years
one could believe they've left

once one is near
there is no room for any others,
each bring their moons
that stay with it forever

the outside does affect inside,
as inside does to outside,
outside can move
the inner planets
change their cycles,
altering spiralling orbits

if planet with name 'Fear' comes near
there's nothing else that one can hear
it's many moons are 'Angst', 'Anxiety'
'Nervousness', 'Insecurity',

'Alarm' and 'Dread', 'Anticipation'
'Apprehension', 'Trepidation'
it often comes with meteorites
that affect all sense of being

time seems to slow,
to drag its feet
each second, like a minute

awareness so unreal
as all is re-tuned, modified
by the pull this planet wields,
good place for fear to be
is in the outer orbits,
if this cannot be done
then move the sun
closer to another one

one planet worthy to be close,
keeps all the others far,
and if your sun does trouble you
merge it with the one,
for it has many treasures,
pleasures,
capacity to sustain life,
to enrich it beyond dreams

such merger affects gravity
and thus each planet's path is changed
and with it their positions

some cannot ideate such bliss
that can build strength from weak
dispel the reverie that seems to reason
the sun's a planet's planet or even less,
a satellite, a follower of misery believing it is destiny

23.Aug 2008

Failed

Once both we shared this feeling,
of love and to belong,
and it brought so much happiness.
Nothing, it seems, went wrong.
As both of us were certain
that this love would not fail.
I'd always thought that love would be
the calm in any gale.

Why did we break apart, I ask? and I hear all your reasons.
And I cannot absorb the words,
for all to have a solution.
Yes, you did love me, that I know,
yet now, as if we'd never known
the closeness that we had, is there

in memory that's aching.

Love is a seed so fragile that it needs a lot of care.
Did we not try to help it grow?
How have we failed it, unaware?
that it took flight and left.

Who is to blame? Just you and I received this gift
and failed to give it everything it needed

and in my thoughts, I'm with you.
I think of you every day.
Hold in my arms, the pillow,
and dream of other days.

27.06 - 20 Oct 2008

Gorge on the flatlands

Inside a gorge,
the days are short
just 12 degrees,
the rest in scattered light.

The view shows sandstone,
granite, boulders,
in all directions
as a cage with one way in,
another out,
the cliffs too steep
to climb.
Each word returns
to those who speak,
the crack of thunder
magnified.

Vision is short,
it fills the eye,

from cliff to cliff,
just as the wave of sound
is trapped,
so is the spirit caught
inside a crack.

The eagles soar as sign
to rise,
up there no walls
to constrain spirit,
except in the unseen flatland canyons,
valleys, gorges,
each with cliffs that reach
2 minutes past the end of time.

31 Aug.2008

Korg

It was the day when ġðʈƠǽỹ
disguised in human form
dwelt amongst the mortal souls.

"What's going on?" it asked the first it came across.
The kid drew a circle in the sand as answer.
ġðʈƠǽỹ nodded, then spoke to the dog,
somewhat uneasy it approached, then walked away.

"What's going on," ġðʈƠǽỹ asked again.
A mountain answered, which had become a road,
crushed into small fragments. "See for yourself,"
the road answered, 'I'm smashed and black with tar.
Once thought I'd live forever, proud and high.'

"What's going on," it asked the river.
The river sent a fish to spit its answer to ġðʈƠǽỹ's face.
It spat it out, "Thank you," it said, "I taste you. You have
changed." The fish spat twice to say: 'We know'.

"What's going on," ġðʈơǽỹ asked the air,
opened its sensors to let it in and quickly let it out again.
"Thanks, but no thanks," ġðʈơǽỹ replied.

Inside a park ġðʈơǽỹ walked to find a bench,
sat down and notices:
"Were you not once a tree? Why hide behind the paint?"
"It's not my doing," said the bench.

ġðʈơǽỹ moved on.

19 Oct 2008

Unseen spirit

The empty page of purity,
no ink yet soaked the fibres in the white …
The canvas bare, as is, unrolled,
not knowing what it's asked to hold …

No sound has echoed from the wall,
soundless is music, before it's born …
The rock unshaped, no chip has flown,
the vision not yet formed to be …

The garden a bare paddock, horse manure
and empty bottles …
The movie before title screen, before budget,
script, long before the thought …

The curtains shut, before the set is build,
the seats are filled, before the actors act …
The dancer's eyes are closed, the body calm,
in waiting, muscles relaxed, before contracting …

Before before, no thought is thought,
no inspiration that inspired, no creation created,
all floats to balance planets with its weight

Before, it comes within our reach to mould,
to shape, to sense the unseen gift,
to give it breath

After before, it is becoming,
a fruit divinely grown,
and on the universal tree
it makes room for new growth to be,
replacing what's been picked or fallen

Before before, and ever after,
each weigh the same in kind,
as unseen substance weighs
a multi-fold of mass of stars and suns combined

Some feel the agony of birthing,
others elated by the same,
and as the moon can lift the tide,
so can unseen celestial clouds
hold on a hundred trillion cells
to lift you up before infusing
gift or curse into the mind

Inside grey soil of neuron paths
creation shapes as seed that's germinating,
as embryonic growth becoming,
coded what it knows to be,
and for a moment the air around will lift
to let you know you're bearing gift

The texture of the word, shaping the sentence,
the colours of the sound, reflecting off the chiselled boulder,
the dancer's shadow echoes from the trees
in the garden that grew to be a park

There is an eye, an ear, a heart, a soul
for all that has become,
that feasts in silent admiration

or smile and cry in understanding
Seen from the furthest distance,
where all suns are mere specks of light,
the unseen spirit of creation
outweighs all seen,
to balance all

No art, and all would fall apart

31 Aug - 1 Sep .2008

The 'Unseen Spirit' of Creation: A Symphony Unfolding

The poem "Unseen Spirit" paints a vivid portrait of the creative process, comparing it to the untouched canvas, the silent stage, and the dormant garden. It delves into the essence of creation, exploring the moments before inspiration takes form and the subsequent transformative journey.

The poem opens with the imagery of an empty page and a bare canvas, symbols of unexplored potential. The purity of the blank canvas signifies the untouched possibilities waiting to be awakened by the unseen spirit of creation.

Soundless music, a rock unshaped, and a garden yet to bloom all echo the silence before the birth of artistic expression.
Capturing the essence of anticipation, the verse elegantly depicts a moment where the prospect of creation lingers in the stillness of the unformed.

The poem weaves a narrative of the movie before the title screen, the curtains shut before the set is built, and the dancer in a state of calm before the performance. Each metaphor emphasizes the unseen spirit's presence before the tangible manifestation of creation.

The concept of 'Before before' introduces a timeless realm where thoughts, inspirations, and creations exist before they come within reach to be shaped. The unseen substance is described as balancing planets with its weight, emphasizing its profound and universal significance.

The poem acknowledges the dual nature of creation, as some experience the agony of birthing, while others revel in the elation of the same process. This duality reflects the varied emotional landscapes involved in the act of creation.

The imagery of the universal tree symbolizes the continuous cycle of creation, growth, and renewal. As new growth replaces what has been picked or fallen, the poem captures the perpetual nature of the creative process.

The unseen spirit is described as having a weight that surpasses the combined mass of stars and suns. This cosmic weight emphasizes the profound impact of the unseen on the visible, shaping and influencing the fabric of existence.

The poet likens creation to a seed germinating inside the grey soil of neuron paths. This metaphor beautifully captures the internal process of shaping an idea, with the moment of revelation lifting the air around, signifying the birth of a gift.

The concluding lines assert the importance of art, suggesting that without it, all would fall apart. The unseen spirit of creation is positioned as a binding force that brings cohesion and balance to the diverse elements of existence.

In essence, 'Unseen Spirit' unfolds as a symphony of creation, orchestrating the journey from potential and silence to the transformative weight of artistic expression. It invites readers to contemplate the unseen forces that shape our world and the immeasurable impact of the creative spirit on the fabric of existence.

no-one said, 'I do'

There was once a town named Some-town
deep inside Some-land,
located east of eastward
in the time zone of some-time.

Each one in the town was Some-one
most of the day they did something,
mostly they never tired
except some of the time.

Further away, a town named Any-town
in the midst of Any-land,
located west of eastward
the time zone there was any-time

Each in the town is Any-one
mostly they did anything
most did never tire
except any of the time

Much further still was No-one
in the land they called No-land,
located west of westward
in the time zone of no-time

Each in the town was No-one
mostly they did nothing
most did never tire
except when there was no-time.

In the west Some-land shared border
with the land called Any-land
and from time to time they argued
where it should start and where to end

Many wars they fought and many times
No-one did invite both
to settle their disputes
and come to No-town in No-land

Someone came to no-one
and any-one came too,
every time they met there was no-time
And no-one did nothing

When they returned, anyone did anything
and some-one did something
That's how it's been since time began
because any-one did anything
and some-one then did something
and no-one did what could be done,
which simply was nothing.

Let's try again, some-one called
any-one did hear it, no-one did nothing.
Any-one was anywhere
and no-one was nowhere,
only some-one was somewhere.

Some-one called for peace
when the others fought
Any-one did the same,
when the others fought
No-one also called for peace,
when the others fought

If no-one joins with some-one they would win,
any-one would lose
If some-one joins with any-one they would win,
no-one would lose
If no-one joins with any-one they would win,
some-one would lose

If any-one joins some-one and no-one,
all would win.
No-one did not agree, suggesting:
If no-one joins any-one and some-one,
all would win
Some-one did not agree, suggesting:
If some-one joins no-one and any-one,
all would win.

Any-one, no-one and some-one did agree on this, all would have
to lose before they could win.

Some-on said, you start then,
any-one said, 'why not you?'
no-one said, 'I do'

3 Sep - 20 Oct 2008

Glued

I am not broken.
I'm glued.

Once broke apart,
but now I'm screwed.

These are not tears,
but oozing glue.

23.09.2007

The Celestial Gaze: Nora's Eyes Trilogy

Relating to the following three works: 'Nora's Eyes' Trilogy:

Part 1: Initial Concerns
In the first part of the trilogy, the narrative revolves around Nora's eyes, which are described as notably large and clear from the day she was born. Her mother expresses concerns about the size of Nora's eyes to Dr. Wilson, who reassures her that it's a normal feature in infants and will likely change as Nora grows older. However, Nora's eyes continue to captivate attention as she gets older.

Part 2: Seeking Professional Advice
The second part introduces Dr. Michael Cameron, an eye specialist, suggesting a growing curiosity about Nora's unique eyes. Nora's aversion to direct eye contact becomes apparent during the consultation, hinting at her discomfort or resistance to scrutiny. Dr. Cameron is perplexed by Nora's eyes but refrains from making any conclusions about her eyesight.

Part 3: Nora's Revelation
In the final part, Nora's perspective is unveiled through her words. Her eyes, described as both a 'gift and curse,' hold a peculiar ability to perceive events beyond the ordinary. Nora speaks of celestial phenomena, referencing her astrological sign (Sagittarius) and describing an approaching cloud that alters the nature of light. Nora seems to possess a heightened awareness, associating colours with emotions and expressing concern for the fate of the celestial bodies.

Themes:

1. Perception and Reality: Nora's eyes challenge conventional perceptions of reality. She seems to perceive celestial events that others cannot, suggesting a unique or heightened sense of awareness.

2. Communication Barriers: Nora's aversion to eye contact and her resistance during the eye examination suggest a difficulty in communication. Her mother tries to understand Nora's perspective, but there is a noticeable gap in understanding between Nora and the adults.

3. Astrology and Symbolism: The use of astrological references, such as Sagittarius, adds a layer of symbolism. Nora's interpretation of celestial events becomes a symbolic language, conveying messages about change, light, and the consequences of celestial interactions.

4. Fear of the Unknown: Nora's distress and fear about the changing celestial events reflect a common human fear of the unknown. Her plea for the archer (Sagittarius) to shoot and prevent the impending change suggests a desire for stability and resistance to the uncertainties of the future.

Overall Impression:
The 'Nora's Eyes' trilogy presents a mysterious and thought-provoking narrative. Nora's unique perspective challenges the boundaries of normalcy, and her ability to perceive celestial events adds an element of fantasy or metaphysical insight. The use of astrology, symbolism, and Nora's cryptic revelations contribute to a story that prompts readers to question the nature of perception, communication, and the mysteries that may lie beyond our immediate understanding.

Nora's eyes (1)

First time she saw the light of day,
we all could see her eyes,
much larger than an infant's eye,
and clear as day.

'Doctor, what's wrong with her?'
her mother asked.
'She's fine, just give her time.'

Nora turned two and loved the sky,
especially at night,
her face lit up in wonderment,
whilst dark it seemed to everyone,
to her it appeared bright.

Two years and six months she was old,
her mum to consult Dr. Wilson,
'Her eyes are still so big,' she said,
'you said they'd change in time.'

'See on this picture, Emily, my first born
on the day she's three,
her eyes don't look like Nora's.'
'What's wrong with her, I need to know.
Her vision is amazing, and often sees
what I can't see, I need to understand.'

'Mrs. Jackson, Nora is your second child, yes, oh, I remember her?'

'Yes, doctor, Emily is my firstborn; she's now 5, and Nora will be 3 in 2 months. I have a picture of Emily, taken when she was three. See for yourself. What is wrong with Nora, doctor? Her eyes are much too big. She looks almost like one of those Japanese cartoon characters.'

'Come here, Nora.'
'Go to the doctor, darling; let him have a look at you.'
'Hello Nora, I'm Dr. Wilson.'
'Hello Wilson,' Nora says.

'She's so adorable; hello, Nora.'

'Mrs. Jackson, all babies have somewhat larger eyes in proportion to adults. It will change as they grow up.'

'That's what you said two years ago. Nora is no longer a baby. She doesn't look anything like Emily at that age, and her vision is amazing.'

What do you mean? the doctor asks. She pulls a 2-inch cube out of her bag, each face containing a letter and a picture. 'Here are the letters A and B and little pictures so that she may get to know the sounds. An apple and a bear, a cat for C and a dog for D, an elephant and a fish, and as you see, they are much smaller than the letters.'

'She doesn't know the letters yet, but she can read the pictures. Let's go out in the corridor, so you'll see for yourself.'

'We stay on this end; take the cube and go right to the end; turn around and show her one face at a time.'

The doctor walks for 20 paces, then stops and turns around.

'No doctor, this is too close; go all the way, right to the end, and when you're there, turn off the light.'

'I'm now at 60 paces.'

'That's good; turn off the light.'

The corridor is dark; the doctor can't be seen.

'Nora, look down there; what can you see?'

'It's Wilson.'

'Can you see a picture on your cube?'

'No.'

'Where is the cube?'

'I don't know.'

'Doesn't Dr. Wilson hold the cube?'

'That I don't know.'

'Look in his hands.'

'Wilson's hands like this', she says, moving her hands behind her back, 'she's hiding hands like this.'

'Show her the cube.'

'Woof, woof, a doggie.' Nora says.

'Is it a D?' her mother questions.

'Wait just a moment; it's too dark.' The light is on, the doctor calls: 'It is,' and studies each face on the cube, and then it's dark again.

Nora points to the darkness and says, 'Fish, fish swimming in the sea; bear, big bear; elephant; apple; dog; I love puss puss; I love she.'

'What animal is puss puss?' her mother asks.

'Cat,' Nora replies, 'she's biscuits all finished; Mummy buy a new one, or puss puss hungry.'

'We will,' she says.

'I love her,' Nora answers.

The light is back on, and the doctor returns, This is extraordinary, I must say. How did you become aware of this?'

'One evening she kept pointing into the dark, calling her cat, Puss Puss, but the cat was right there with us. Next morning I found her cube, 100 metres from the door, showing the letter C. You can see how small the picture of the cat is; at 100 metres, I would be lucky to see the cube in daytime, let alone the small picture in the dark.'

'I'm not at all concerned about her eyesight, rather the opposite. It seems that Nora can see things that are invisible to me or any other member of the family. I can see it in her behaviour. On occasion, while walking along a park, she has stopped and refused to go any further. If I insist on going on, she will cry, which quickly turns into a screaming rage, like an overpowering fear. She will calm down as soon as we walk in the other direction, but she can't tell me what she sees.

'But that's not what I came to show; she speaks, and I can't grasp the essence of her meaning. Perhaps you know. Nora, my darling girl, tell Dr. Wilson of the flames that you saw behind your sign.'

'In Sagitrus, the flame is dying; the dark is eating it,' says Nora.

'She means to say Sagittarius, her sign of birth, which she knows well. What does she mean by that?'

'Please, Nora, tell me more of this, why does the dark eat flames?' asks Dr. Wilson.

'That I don't know. Sagitrus was pretty and now it's not the same, the dark moved in the flame,' she says, 'the other day the flame, like this, so big it was, so pretty, and now it's dark and Sagitrus is sad.'

'What colour was the flame before?'
She points at her dress, the part that's red, 'like this', she said, 'the flame got heavy and it fell, not all of it but some. That's why pretty Sagitrus is sad, it falling and then it gone.'
'The light is heavy, that is why it falls into the sky.'

'But light does not weigh anything, where can it fall to, do you know?'
'The flame got heavy, then it fell back home,' she says.

'How did the light get heavy?'
'When it flew across a growing cloud, none like it ever I had seen.
'The light slowed down just as a fish in mud could no longer travel, as mud slows waves and makes them stop. From where the cloud came, I don't know, but it is coming closer as it grows. It seems to seek the light, and when they meet, a change occurs.'

Nora's eyes (2)

'Mrs. Jackson, I would like to send you a referral to a colleague of mine, an eye specialist, Dr. Michael Cameron. There is certainly nothing wrong with Nora's eyesight, but I have never come across anything like it. Dr. Cameron's clinic is near the roundabout. Is she allowed candy?
'No, please don't, but thank you.'

--|--

Two days after her 3rd birthday, Nora is in Dr. Cameron's clinic. Her first impression of Dr. Cameron was negative, and it would not change throughout the consultation. 'No looking at me,' she'd say, the eyepiece apparatus on his head more of a hindrance than an aid. The closer he came, the more Nora withdrew. Eventually, she closed her eyes and refused the examination.

'Nora, Dr. Cameron just wants to look into your eyes,' Mrs. Jackson said.

'I know,' she peeked, 'stop looking at me.'

'Do you have any children?' asked Mrs. Jackson. 'No, I don't,' he answered. Nora's eyes are now firmly shut. No amount of coaxing would open them.

5.10.2008

Nora's eyes (3)

Nora is three, her gift and curse
large eyes of colour brown.
None understood the words she said,
'Archer is sad.
Light is not light, but heavy,
that's why it falls into the sky.'

Born out of Virgo,
silent cloud
none like it ever been,
of substance stranger than is known,
with powers yet unseen.

Towards the archer's flame it seeks
to feed there what it finds
and while it does
it sheds its weight and grows.

The Sagittarian flame is doomed
despite far distance from the cloud,
this Nora's eyes could see

as it approached her sign of birth.

Cloud it was none,
more like a sheet,
a thinnest sieve of sorts,
yet objects pass unnoticed
changing none but one.

It feeds the light,
the photon's weight increased
to slow its path.
The waves cease travel
as if near muddy shores.

All light must fall,
as heavy light is going to be dark.
The beams of light
feed sheet to grow
in size and in dimension.
Transforms,
from sheet to cube it grows
the more it sheds its weight.

Nora begs the archer, 'shoot,
else it will change your flame'
it gains in speed and size,
and light falls in its wake.

Archer too far, sound far too slow
to ever reach at all,
too weak her voice
left with no choice she weeps
for it may lose its flame.

Sagittarius without red,
Nora's big eyes turn sad.
'My pretty archer cannot hear,
he'll lose the colour in his flame.

Turn 'round and shoot!
Why does he not?
It grows and will come closer.
Perhaps he's out of arrows.
The light will fall into the sky.'

'But Nora, dear, how can it be?'
her mother asks the girl.
'It's true, Mama, you'll see.
But when you do
you won't see me
or anything at all.'

9-12 Oct 2008

The Planet

The day began when it was night,
much deeper than the depth of sight.
In 15 seconds, all would change.
the sky no eye had seen.

Three bodies on a collision course
with planet Blue, the first will miss,
but not the other two,
9 seconds left of bliss.

The first deflected from its path.
spew trailing debris in its wake.
The next will not be kind; it hits.
The last of the bodies slams in side
to split the planet into bits
to shudder planet to its core,
and plume of black will fail to rise.

21 Oct 2008

Flying

the jets hum smooth
the stress of take off past,
the earth's birth of release,
shielded from my memory.

Mother below,
round is your belly,
still incubating more to try
to reach for heaven,
but many fly just to the sky.

Vision set forth,
rushing, clouds wiz by
yet I feel as on solid ground
the plane's floor built
to give impression
that it would not fail.

And whilst accelerating fast
it feels as if I'm standing still
no matter where
the destination's dial is set
there's stillness
as if suspended,
yet proof is otherwise.

Point of arrival based on point
of leaving, time and strain,
fuel spent on any comfort
may shorten distance gained.

24 July 2008

taking

taking - giving
passing on
passing through
passing by
passing
pass
pass across
pass around
pass on

26.July 2008

anywhere is now

from - to
past - future
anywhere is
here - now

26. July 2008

Tiny seeds

Tiny are the seeds of life,
in abundance everywhere,
yet fragile each
and precious all,
to take never for granted.

16 Oct 2008

Before the dawn

I want to wake inside your hand,
curl in your warmth, your touch, your care
to hold your head so near
blow sweetest breath right through your hair,
into your ear,
to whisper, 'Dear, wake up, it's time'

Before the sun has chance to throw
its radiating rays
from deep below the oceans crest
both, us, with sleepy eyes
bring coffee in a jar,
walk through the sand,
half dressed, to rest,
there, arm in arm

Watch soldier crabs do exercise
and guard us from all preying eyes
while others rolling balls of sand aside,
we see horizon's colours greet
the coming of the day

Between my legs you sit, embraced,
I hold, oh, you so close to me
with both arms wrapped around you,
together, look towards the east across the sea

Just as the sun breaks through
the glimmering ocean's peaks,
I watch the first ray fast approaching
catch it, before it hurts your eye, I say,
'My Dear, you're so beautiful today'

Your eyes to squint, I move aside,
to rest your body on the sand
have never seen a breast
in golden morning light
kissed by the sun and I

'Oh, Dear, do you hear this?'
'The gentle whispers of the sea,
that tiny little wavelets bring,
as if they're watching us and grin'
while we make love as one to greet the sun

Filled with a smile that lovers know
the inner calm you bring,
the music of each word you say,
each sound you hush,
each touch you brush,
kiss softly every part of you,
this oh so special time we're in
I thank the sun for shining onto you

'Up there, up high, you see the dot?'
'Day soon will hide the star'
and then we both remember
the coffee in the jar
and sip, and moist your lips
gloss in the light, invite another kiss

'Say, Dear, have you heard the sound?'
'Yes, waves and birds and whispers'
'No louder, much, much louder than...'
'Oh yes, I did, my heart and yours
and both our breath in harmony'

'Oh yes, but no, much louder, sharper, like a bang,
before the sun came up?'

'Don't think I did, my Love'

Perhaps another dawn
'Which sound my Love?'
'The crack of dawn?'

And then we laugh in knowing
that dawns wake peacefully
wherever we will be
together

© Heinz Ross, Gold Coast, Australia, 27 Jan 2009

---

bliss

in serenading bliss
the do's that don't will miss
the ideals they believe in
cannot give a kiss

© Heinz Ross, Gold Coast, Australia, 4 Jan 2009

Next

Did not expect to find you here,
how have you been?
When did you leave?

     Five years ago, next Monday,
     I'm fine, thank you for asking.

Tell me, what will I find behind the doors?
     Relax, you will see soon enough.
Come-on, I need to be prepared,
what do they know about me?

     A little late for that, I think,
     they know more than you can recall.
Oh dear, it's curtains then for me.

     'Next', the speaker on the desk announced,

it's your turn, please, let me assist you.

  I am OK, I'll manage it.
  Have I not always done before?
I did not know you well enough before,
my views don't count.

    Please come inside, sit down.

  Hello.

    We don't make idle conversations,
    please do restrain from such.

  Sorry.

    There's time for that after we show you
    what you should be sorry for,
    if that's your choice of course.
    How many enemies of yours
    have you turned into friends?
    How many of the friends you had
    changed sides?

  Oh, let me think

    Don't bother,
    it's 0
    and the second answer's 49.

  That could be close.

    Not close, that is the answer,
    period.

14.Oct 2008

Letters in the ink

In the pot of ink the letters in a knot,
immersed within,
liquefied,
inseparable,
all as one

Scribe tries to extract one with reed,
reed cannot hold the ink,
ink splatters on the page
to leave in spotted pattern
sentence in a blob

22 Apr 2009

Treads

Most still remember you
for you spoke softly, calmly, quietly,
for you walked silently,
with each step treading gently.
Dressed in the coat of poverty,
each could fill from your riches
they all did sense you had.

Most remember you
as the one with strength,
despite apparent weakness,
that you carried in your frail body,
who's silence was a call,
who's actions mirror of your words
who's lived amongst his own and all.

They know you still and weep,
your humility a sign
of your humanity.
They saw and knew,
you're one of them,
but also so much more,
but that you never said.

You lived your message,
humbly,
no false pride,
your head bowed low to each you met,
to make each feel as king
discovering own self-worth.

And the lower you kneeled,
they too began to raise the other.
Beneath the smallest
you lowered your head,

to show your respect,
to help restore identity
and so did they in time greet others.
The more you minified yourself,
the more you grew in their eyes.

They reached for your hand,
they searched for your eye,
you helped them believe they could,
and then they knew it too,
and they did.

And all you did is love them.
They didn't know, it was so rare.
Because you gave your love
they followed you.

The perception of a day changed
by knowing you were amongst them.
And they had strength to bear all hardship,
the light of hope lit in their eyes.

Many could not grow to become,
for whatever reason,
as much as they wanted to.
Have they failed you?

Strength, solutions, harmony, peace,
all contained in love.
It was so easy to believe with you near,
so hard to fathom, without.

One man of integrity
inspiring most to seek tomorrow
filled with anticipation.
Enriched in knowing that
`they can't' became `they can'.

In love rendered defenceless
against Cain's legacy,
you died as mortal being.
For many the journey stopped,
as they were followers of you,
instead of what you brought them.

Most returned
to follow their own path
in endless circles
where they had been before.

And some dared
to step upon the first tread
of the steps of love.
Some brought their safety railing
until they could let go.

Many feared to fall.
Despite the height,
despite the danger,
each tread in love
is safe as solid ground.

31.July 2008 - 31.Aug. 2008

Between eternities

Between eternities,
a state of finite being,
two cells united start dividing,
grow into a living form.

Cell clusters an abode of one,
apart from others
as in cells of isolating prisons,
each alone not knowing
why one had become.

All are alike, yet each unique,
dwell in sphere
none else can share,
each to own its point of view,
different from all others.

Between eternities
one's quest to live to die,
be that as virus, fish or tree
each part of family, as I.

In time with end
however long or short
some hasten to return, or hope
extending lifespan beyond time.

Is life the place to settle score?
as life eternal won't allow,
a chance to hide from pain in death,
escaping agony to rest?

Perhaps temporal state,
to gain in growth of spirit,
reborn in countless combinations,
until eternal timelessness
abates the need of living.

But die we do still whilst we're living,
shed and grow in constant change,
there cannot be eternity
whilst living breast is breathing.

Yet all I am has been before
and will remain thereafter
in timeless transformation
of eternal entity.

20-21 Oct. 2008

Ephemeral Odyssey: Between Eternities

Amidst the vast expanse between eternities, a finite existence emerges—a union of two cells embarking on the journey of division, evolving into a living entity. These clusters of cells form individual abodes, akin to isolated prisons, each unaware of the reasons behind their singular existence.

Though uniform in essence, each entity is inherently unique, residing within its own sphere of perception, distinct from all others. The ceaseless cycle of life unfolds—a quest to exist, to perish, whether as a virus, fish, or tree, all interconnected as part of a larger family.

In the passage of time, some eagerly embrace the return to the eternal unknown, while others seek to prolong their existence, navigating the delicate balance between life and death. Is life a mere battleground for settling scores, or does eternal life deny respite from the pain of mortality?

Perhaps this temporal state serves as a crucible for the growth of the spirit, a transient journey through countless combinations until the yearning for living dissipates in the timeless embrace of eternity. Yet, even within the realms of living, transformations persist—a constant shedding and regrowth, as breath lingers within the rhythm of life.

Though we may question the prospect of eternity while our mortal breath persists, the essence of who we are transcends temporal boundaries. Existing in a state of timeless transformation, the eternal entity within us persists beyond the boundaries of before and after.

Kitten

it is said,
perhaps too, written,
that each cat was once a kitten
could turn some, becoming bitter
cause their offspring's name is 'litter'

22 Oct 2008

No time for dreams

Harry loved fishing in the ocean,
wanting a boat for years.
hard
to get his dream,
and then it stood
unused for years,
too ill he was, then
death got in the way
dream of fishing may have changed
his destiny, boat left,
not knowing what to do

James, for years wrapped in a dream
maker of films, directing,
he saw his name in lights
spent years for it preparing
and when he had it all
he never had a script.

Divorce and heart attack,
he's dead
than all his stuff sold for a dime

Jerry's dream to build a firm,
moving heavy loads.
From one truck grew to eight,
had special loaders there as well.
Once could not pay a bill on time
that set the wheels in motion,
auctions, repossession,
knocks on the door

He lost all that he ever made.
All trucks taken, loaders too,
including house and home,
too late,
but he survived
with damaged pride
and takes it easy now

Sarah trapped in debt,
'I shall be happy when I'm free.'
Sally in need of love,
'I'd be happy finding him or he finds me.'
Pilgrim aches, 'I shall be glad,
to reach where I am going.'
The climber reached the summit,
on descent he slips
descending to the never been

Mary lived a dream,
she didn't need to reach,
it was always there,
never had time to dream

24 Oct 2008

Tanker / Sailor

Calm waters, vessel powers smoothly
cuts the waves with ease
Cabins set below the helm,
bridge far back, near stern it rising
crew have windows facing forward
bow 500 yards ahead
I'm a sailor for this voyage
met the guys, try to be crew

bearded silent bear sits smoking
pipe and views the fore-deck's empty space
'Let's have a look,' says I, he moves,
fore-deck big as a soccer field,
great place to kick a ball

He laughs and coughs and blows his smoke
straight into my face,
'Sorry kid' he mutters.
'Why's he watching this all day?'
I ask to hear one say,
'He just likes blue, that's why.'

Feel though like the odd one out,
first day, not part of them
Admire vessel's smooth design,
radii around the superstructure,
watertight bond, fore-deck to hull
nothing is sharp, all smooth and new,
yellowish green the outer coats,
inside is white and clean

Get into port of call,
load up cargo of who knows what,
then head out through the white capped wash
storm right head, we're facing

swells rising, vessel still cutting peaks
until it's further out sea
things somewhat change

Some cabins forward, in the bow,
I'm told to get there now,
the vessel movement side to side
upward, downwards,
long way to go
and when I get there
'here I am'
'yeah, this is not the place to be, go back'
Once back, the old bear still smoking pipe as calm
the other crew play deck of cards
'Let's have a look,' ask bear to shift
he does, no blue in sight
just grey water from streaming clouds
until the bow goes down

And there a wall of surf,
10 times the size of tubes I saw
out in mid ocean, holy crap
that thing is coming down
the bow digs in, the fore-deck gone
the window foams with froth
the crew all hands on deck of cards
so they don't move

I don't believe these guys,
that's why I'm still the odd one out.
I had seen cats split into bits
on less than this is taking
what if..., which way is out
one never knows, if I should ask,
they'll surely will be laughing,
but I don't care, sailor I am
but only for this trip.
20 Nov 2008

Siberian spring

Forest in transformation
seasonal change,
grey reveals some specks of green
sunset in orange glow
approaching night will still be cold
as yellow flame is dancing
the glow to radiate a ring of warmth
I throw another log and watch
the sparks disperse
into the fading day

My eye to scan the contours of the trees
the trunks are closer to the night
into the flicker, drawn to dream
until I'm wide awake from fright
What's that,
in front of me?

Slowly approaching, lone male wolf,
low posture, careful, inching, judging,
ready it, to spring to life
shivers crawl on my back
around my neck

within fraction of second see
another time
when black and two greys chased
from pack of six and circled,
plenty of scars
yet somehow did survive

I clear my eyes, adjust to darkness
and in the glow of flames I see its head
blood red its snout, but longer than a wolf,
head as greyhound, Tassie tiger cross,

or so it seems.
The winter coat begins to shed
grey, whitish fluffy clouds of down,
each branch will help to brush it off
what stupid thing to notice
with a wolf 10 yards away

Such striking head and shades
of dark-red blend to copper near its tail
It could look fierce
but does not growl
the night silent, no howls,
is it alone?

Red wolf's eyes heavy, slow approach, tail flat
not like a threat or is it cunning?
distrust we both go through
closer it moves,
each paw testing the limit,
gauge reactions
head low down,
yet breath too hot for calm

My heart beats near my ear so loud
can barely hear exhaling sound
yards from the fire it hesitates
and waits for what I do
I sit with caution
hum a tune;
eye the flaming log of use,
well, just in case

I see its teeth; I see its tongue,
the heat free to escape,
ears folded back
can barely trust my eyes
as wolf lays near the fire, calm,
looks to the flames

head turned to tend its hind leg.
I look around, is he alone
or is the pack right in my back?
All set in eerie calm
yet too, serene

Inner turmoil of fear or hope
what does it want
from me?

What have you done?
Caught by a trap, a swollen leg,
three times the normal size
we need to try to get it off you

If we can trust another
there's a chance

Stay calm, it's not a dog.
I hum my tune a little louder
as not to have my fear as near
its ears rotate whilst eyes as heavy as before

My hand now slowly reaches out,
it growls and so do I
it stops I hum instead
my left hand holds part of the trap
its head reaches my hand to sniff

daps with its tongue
so far so good

my other hand now holds the second half
slowly I strain to ease the clamping jaws of trap
Wolf's getting restless,
easy now,
...and then the leg is free

© Heinz Ross, Gold Coast, Australia, 1 Nov 2008

Once spoke

Once spoke,
each word still echoes,
carries pain of then,
draws in agonising beauty colours
that none else could claim

soothing sounds of want
weaving web of longing still
yearning that which evades

What's it like, to wake up dead?

I guess the worst thing that can happen,
you wake up
to find you're dead,
and suffering caffeine starvation
you're not aware of it just yet.

At six o'clock, the day begins
you lift the blanket, swing your legs
and as you stand beside the mattress
you left yourself behind, still sleeping,
there in bed.

Oh, what a feeling that must be
who am I and who is he?
I thought I went alone to bed,
who then is he that looks like me?

I need my coffee first of all,
so that my eyes can focus,
so that my heart keeps beating
and then will think of what to do.

I pour the water in the jug,
the jug's not moving,
nothing's dripping from the spout.
No matter how I move the lever
it is still there where it was found.

Let's check the bathroom,
brush the teeth
splash some moisture in my face,
enable me to face the day,
oh what a waste.

I must be out of water,
just as well, no need for towel,
got no water anyway.

I have just learned a new trick,
walking through the door.
Why does it have a handle with a lock?
What for?

Oh, what a day this 's going to be
without the coffee starting me,
without a splash to clear my eyes
is the heart still beating? No.
I'm not surprised!

The phone starts ringing, what to do?
I was going to say, 'Hold on'
to who may ring this hour of the day
but couldn't lift the dooby up to say,
'there will be some time delay.'

Let's analyse the situation,
let's get a grip of what goes on.
The heart's on strike,
as is the water
and who was that
still in my bed?

I move towards the place of resting
try new things, through the wall,
just testing,
easy as,
that saves some walking,
he's still asleep as I walk in.

'Hey you, hey me, hey I,' I call, but hear no voice
I clap my hands but must have missed
can hear no sound or hiss.
I move his shoulder,
it does not
am I awake, asleep, forgot.

If he is I, then better listen,
am I snoring in my sleep,
is he, I mean?
He's not,
that's good,
because I knew that I don't snore.

Of course, no heartbeat helps conserve
a lot of energy one needs
to keep the system going.
It's just one quickly tires
as everything is slowing.

Once I am truly rested
perhaps the water works again,
and start the day afresh,
freshly brewed coffee
as a friend

I think I go to bed
and have a nap instead
'til then.

Flowers are...

Flowers are the reflection of an eye,
the answer to a sigh
a tissue for a cry,
the word that answers 'why'

7 Nov2008

---

she said

truck labours up the stretching hill
past peak the downhill run
as weight adds speed
change from the outer to the centre lane
to take the truck in front

both overtaking lanes are clear
the slow ones carry heavy traffic
Five lanes reduce to three
in just 2 miles from here

past truck and signal change of lane
rear mirror shows all clear
truck now in second lane,
tanker up front,
low loader right behind

rear mirror shows a battle
high beams flash from afar,
two nuts play high speed games
5 lanes, now 4, in 80 yards be 3
both are still undecided,
who is to give an inch?
The outer pushes the inner
between tanker and the truck
he's sliding in and blows a tire

truck slows,
low loader tries,
too much momentum, smoking brakes
and melting rubber forming clouds
a proper mess
when wheels did come to rest

driver of low loader to grabs a wrench
in anger runs forward
truck driver with steel bar
ready to smash one of the idiots head in

11 Nov 2008

full of promise

Full of promise
full of possibility
barren page
plain white
no thought yet captured to convey

13 Nov 2008

Impossible

There is no way to fight poverty,
wage war against hunger,
no way to fight for peace.
One cannot declare war on drugs
or a global war against unemployment,
injustice, terror, fear.

One cannot use the language of hate
for a noble cause,
it is simply IMPOSSIBLE.

14 Nov 2008

Shepherd

It was on the day I first saw you
you could have picked any of us
when you saw me, your hand reached out
I came and you said, 'wow'
I think that was the start
when I began to love you

I was overcome in knowing
that you thought I was special,
kinked, floppy ears you didn't mind
and short rat's tail, feet much too large
my mother's owner handing you
the lineage of my breed

Sire and Dames, high pedigree
of old foundation bloodlines
Level 1, strong head, yet even temper
rich black and tan, not yet, too young
I licked your hands, you stroked my coat
then we left all my siblings

First time I slept foot end of bed,
a bed I never ever had,
your toes do wriggle in your sleep,
perhaps you are just dreaming

You fed me from an orange bowl,
and when I piddled on the wall
you yelled and chucked me out the door
in time I'd learn and scratched instead

Ten months I stayed inside the house
and could not help the shedding
of winter coat and clouds of fur
as summer came to be

You built a cage for me
and when you could you let me out
together we would walk the tracks
I could delight in running free
never too far though from your feet

And every time you did come close
my heart in joyous jubilation
I pushed as close as I could go
to feel the warmth of your affection

You loved me still, that's all I needed
just a look, that will sustain, that will remain
that be the company I have
as snow and ice are cold,
the thought of you so nice to hold
if just in memory at night,
or when you're gone for weeks

Are you still sore that I did growl?
That I did bite defending,
are still upset me bringing down
the man who raised his arm?

He tried to hurt you, so it seemed,
no-one dare hurt the one I love,
I run through fire, anything,
guard all your things and all your love
and bear all that I'm asked to bear,
desert you I can never

oh dear, what have I done to you,
sense nothing good is coming
despite I come close to your feet
wriggle my tail and hope you feel
that I can make you love me too

The lash of whip I feel as pain
not understanding why you do,
something that happened
to who knows
or made you feel,
it's not my doing

hit me again, break I may do,
but once the love I gave is true,
no change that I feel towards you
but let your rage free reign

Don't hit the black, the black's asleep
better to let it slumber
as in the tan the one you know I am,
black is the wolf within

Merry-go-round

The pain I got returning
as pay-back for your wrong
and as the child before me
can't grasp that you're long gone
and so he too will find me
after I fade away
in some poor kid
that's no idea
the merry-go-round we're on

The fire of love

The earth is flat
the earth is round
and if it's round it can be both
go gather wood, we need it

the sky a flat sheet with a hole
and many smaller ones as well
each moving one direction
different speeds for some,
behind, the mother photon fused
its babies

fuse is the word, spread out,
some kindling too we need

Hear this, the earth is neither,
not flat, nor round, but sphere
as if reflecting rays of light
float on the watery skin of
bubbles blown from soap and water
their inside filled with air, so too
the continents float on the inside
of spherical bubble,
hence the air cannot escape
each living with a problem throws it away
and so it hits another on the head

go forth and cut the forests down
need all the wood that we can get
the straight ones raise as poles
one end set in the ground

Hear this, the earth is sphere
continents swim, yet without sinking
the earth is cube, we all know that
the earth is tube,
how could it be?
the earth multifaceted shape
grown from the difference in opinion

how many poles we need?
set one for each

see all the different kinds of wood
none is alike, rich textures, grain and density
tolerance is a forest
but now we've cut it down

Each tie another to a pole
both, on the wrists and ankles

The earth is

is what?
is is enough

Who can tie me?
none there to tie me on the pole,
as all are tied
I'll help to tie you

Is the earth?

The Earth is love
impossible
love has no contradictions
no high and low,
no cold and hot,
no wet and dry

Love is a spark
made from a stick of life,
a tree is life
two lives make love
like this, drill one hard stick
into another, softer,
turn one, the other heats
there is the spark
blow gently, give it life
born as a flame, this is the purity of love

three things love needs
if it is flame
part of life or of life once lived,
heat, and the breath of life, that's it
and in consuming purify
the heretics within

That is correct, the flame of love
ignite the kindling first
and then the gathered wood that's stacked under your feet,
to reach in loving arms
towards you, all embracing,
purity be that's left

Are we to burn as heretics?
The flame of love cannot consume you otherwise.

I'm glad to know, go throw your flame
my trust be in the flame of love,
and so is mine, me too, and I,
bring flame to kindling we prepared

The flame thrown to the kindling,
ignites around a ring of fire
singe the constrains on legs and arm,
all free to go, none moves away,
each standing firm, holding their pole

if there is heretic within, then burn it out,
so let it be
one to the other smiles and knows,
united in a ring of love
can never cause us agony

Two hours pass, all still alive,
day turned to night
the one who threw the flame is cold
all others stand on glowing warmth

Dead trees unable to breathe out,
even at night cannot give life
the flame must die
the smouldering glow gives warmth
charcoal be left

Each steps from piled up corpse of trees
to thank the thrower of the flame
loving embrace to share their warmth
with one who shivers needing

The flames of love are gone,
dead trees are not in need
yet in each heart forever
love does not know defeat

© Heinz Ross, Gold Coast, Australia, 28 Nov 2008

Harmony's Ember: 'The Fire of Love'

In 'The Fire of Love,' the poem explores diverse perceptions of the Earth's shape, intertwining them with the multifaceted nature of love. From the tangible acts of gathering wood to the metaphorical tying of individuals to poles, the poem weaves a narrative that culminates in the symbolic ignition of the flame of love.

The verses begin by presenting contrasting views of the Earth's shape, blending flatness, roundness, and various other forms. This mirrors the diverse opinions and perspectives that individuals hold in society, shaping the narrative of collective existence.

The act of tying individuals to poles serves as a metaphor for the constraints and bonds that society imposes. However, the poem suggests a collective agreement to be bound together, fostering unity despite the differences.

The poem introduces a profound idea that the Earth embodies the essence of love. It explores love as an entity free from contradictions, analogous to the purity of a flame. The metaphorical act of igniting love symbolizes the transformative power of this emotion.

The poem breaks down the components necessary for the flame of love: heat, the breath of life, and the ability to consume impurities within. This imagery suggests that love has the power to purify and unite, transcending individual differences.

The act of throwing a flame onto kindling, creating a ring of fire, becomes a communal ritual. This ritual symbolizes the shared warmth of love that binds individuals together, eradicating the metaphorical heretics within and fostering a sense of togetherness.

As the flame subsides and the dead trees turn to charcoal, the poem reflects on the transient nature of the flame of love. However, it emphasizes that the warmth and essence of love persist within each heart, leaving an enduring mark.

The concluding scenes depict a shared warmth among individuals, transcending differences and fostering unity. The poem asserts that the flames of love, though extinguished, leave an indelible imprint, forever present in the collective consciousness.

In essence, 'The Fire of Love' is a poetic exploration of unity, love, and the enduring impact of shared warmth, symbolized by the transformative power of a flame that kindles and purifies.

Fear

The sun fills your shade as soon as you let it
The wind fills your wings as soon as you fly
But the flatland eagles that never dared
scared when sparrow's shadows rush by

it

fail in describing it by word
shall keep its innocence unspoiled
un-watched it dwells in silent bliss
nameless it needs no guard, nor hide,
as sounds approaching stop sign halt
in silence dwell silently
unrevealed 'it' free of name,
it unaware of gift received
left as a question rests
shapeless letters forming words

shade-less colours void of spectrum
trying to describe unknown
silence fuels word's starving ache
refusing it to prosper

Emptiness

a glass filled with emptiness
cannot spill,
remains filled,
as long as emptiness fills its surrounds
try as you will
one cannot fill
a glass with emptiness
that's not empty to fill
unless non-empty content spills.

So what

Speaker spoke, none there to listen,
words floating, seeks an ear to hear

Seer saw, could not explain,
so eyes could picture seen,
not even Argus chanced a glimpse

Walker walked, yet never moved,
walked 'round in circles
earth turning underneath

Dreamer dreamt, but could not catch,
consciousness blinding depth

Thinker thought, though thought though
different, but this each thought is by default

Heinz Ross
28 Nov 2008

sunrise

Are birds still singing from your trees,
the gums still swaying in the breeze,
sunrise to make your curtains glow
flooding your room in golden light

31 Jan, 2010, Bam

Milk (Trigger warning: Loss)

(Infants can't talk, but if they could, perhaps that's what would be said.)

Hush baby now
no need to cry
it is the hunger, that is all
come take my left,
's not much, but some,
enough to ease
'til cramps are gone
hush baby dear
and if you can
hide in some sleep

Mama, Mama,
my mouth is full
but this I cannot swallow
what are you feeding me?
Mama,
your breast tastes not the same

Hush baby, drink
it's warm, it's rich
it's all you need to have
it has all what your body wants
not much, but best
that I can give

Mama, I cannot swallow this

this is not milk you're giving
it's something else,
I don't know what,
but milk it's not
Mama, please stop

Drink, darling please,
don't waste a drop
my milk takes time to make
the other I'll keep for tonight
that's when you need it too

Mama, I must let this milk flow
out from my mouth so...
Don't close my nose,
how can I breathe?

Forgive me, child, I had to do
or you'd have spat it out
I'm glad you got it down
your belly will be pleased

It's not, Mama, it's not
can you not feel I'm pleading
I am so sick and tired
this pain much stronger than before

How is my grandson warrior?
Oh Mum, he wants to spit it out
I don't know what is wrong with him
What do you think it could be?

But look, his mouth is blue and green
what have you done to him?
He's barely breathing, quickly, speak
What have you given him?

Nothing, Mother, I fed him this,

my left, to calm his hunger
But look, he's fading fast,
what can I do, what do I do?

Don't shake the babe,
give him to me
I turn him over and you help,
Do as I say

Now, gently tap his back
What are you doing to my son?
I said to gently tap his back,
a little stronger now
not with your fingers,
use flat hand,

once more, that's it
and here it comes,
come boy,
just get it out

Thank you Mother, he is alive,
beautiful sound, a baby's cry

What did you say he had?
Your breast?
Inside his belly, he had this.
This is not milk, what did you give this boy?

I swear to God, he had my breast
that's all I gave to him
Which one?
This one, there's not much left

Squeeze some into my hand
It does look odd somehow,
squeeze more

This is not mothers' milk
cannot describe the taste
but it's causing me all sorts of pain

What did you drink, what did you eat?
Some reeds along the river,
I too shall try, this milk I have
it does taste strange

Mother your mouth turns colour,
your neck is swelling
And so is yours,
your mouth as well,
what have we done to us,
who will be with the child?

Jester's lot (Trigger warning: Loss)

the jester does the deed
has them in stitches, fills their need
and on the sun-drenched stone they dance;
none of his tears evaporate

they hold their bellies, clap and cheer
forget themselves and all their fears
grotesque the mirror that reflects
their agony in laughter

and with their weight upon his back
his tears in streams colour stone black
and slip he must, then breaks his neck
to their applause, 'good show,' they said

and on his body throw their coins
none knows that eight kids lost the voice
that dad left each night in their ear
so they may never know to fear

© Heinz Ross, Gold Coast, Australia, 10 Jan 2009

Beyond the Verses: Understanding 'The Jester's Lot'

'The Jester's Lot' intricately navigates the delicate interplay between public performance and private tragedy. Through vivid imagery and evocative language, the narrative unfolds to portray a jester whose outward exuberance masks profound inner turmoil.

The opening lines establish the jester's dual role, portraying him as one who 'does the deed' and 'fills their need,' signifying a performer meeting audience expectations. The sun-drenched stone serves as a symbolic stage where the jester's tears dance, a poignant metaphor for his internal struggles, enduring despite the heat that would dissipate ordinary tears.

The audience's response, manifested in belly-holding laughter and applause, attests to the jester's success in diverting attention from personal anguish. The mirror reflecting their 'agony in laughter' creates a powerful image, highlighting the paradox of deriving joy from another's suffering.

As the poem unfolds, the jester's burden becomes palpable, symbolized by the weight on his back—the audience's approval proves insurmountable. The lines 'his tears in streams colour stone black, and slip he must, then breaks his neck' describe a literal and metaphorical fall. This tragic turn is juxtaposed with the callous 'good show' from the audience, who remain oblivious to the jester's real-life tragedy, perceiving it as just another act.

The concluding lines unveil the hidden cost of the jester's performance—the loss suffered by his eight children. The audience's obliviousness, contrasted with the intimate knowledge of the children, underscores the isolation and loneliness borne by those who entertain. The poem concludes with a poignant reflection on the children's potential ignorance of their father's pain, emphasizing the disconnect between public perception and private reality.

The revelation that the audience interprets the jester's demise as part of the act deepens the tragedy. This stark contrast between the public facade of entertainment and the personal tragedy faced by the jester adds poignancy to the narrative, intensifying the theme of hidden pain behind a mask of performance.

In essence, 'The Jester's Lot' delves into the sacrifices made by those who bring joy to others, illustrating the poignant irony of a performer whose personal tragedy remains unnoticed amid applause. The poem prompts reflection on the masks individuals wear, the burdens they carry in silence, and the profound impact of unacknowledged sorrow.

Burden Day (Trigger warning)

It's 'Burden Day', the sign declared,
scheduled for a Wednesday.
A strong young man who volunteered,
to be the driver for this year.

The truck stretched long, from here to there,
the back tray empty, clean and bare.
The young boy knew no fear but laughed,
this his first 'Burden' run.

Sally, relieved to hear the sound,
waiting since sunrise, so as not to miss.
Her worry-box near bursting at the seams.
She dropped it in the truck and screamed,
with joy, so pleased.

A kid, next door, approached the driver,
"Never I've done this before."
"Don't worry, son," the driver said,
"we place your burden near the door."

Eyesore with yellow wooden shutters,
housing a family of generations three.
Nine kids they had, plus one.
The driver asked, "What have you got for me?"
Dad shook his head, Mom said: "Got none."

The Miller's place near blocked the road,
with burden left and centre.
They all chipped in to load the truck
and wished the driver well, and luck.

The truck did stop at fifty-nine,
the cottage at the rear.
The man walking the garden path
found Gwandoya drinking,
though not drunk.

"Where is the burden
that I came to take away?"
Gwandoya resting his head
on both hands, replied,
"The burden's all in here."
"It's liquid slush inside my brain,
that is my burden and my pain."

"No worries," said the driver,
"what we will do is this,
we drain the pain out of your ears
into the bottles here."

Two dozen full, plus three, one short,
"What do we do?" he asked Gwandoya.
"Drain the one with Port."

As he returned to find the truck,
he barely could distinguish what it was.
The wheels flat from the load,
the back-tray filled with Burden.

The roof deformed,
as more heaped upon more,
even the bonnet overflowing.

Two skeletons from cupboards,
tied to the truck with strings,
two plastic bags of worries
and a note to come again.

End of the road is Marge, last stop.
Wheelchair-bound for years, she said,
"Would have thought they let a young man drive,"
as he drank her salty pearls.

"I was," said he, "this morn."
"Have thanks," said she,
"the road beyond 's not easy."

(27/28.10.2007)

---

inner universe

inside is as the outside
distance inverted
short space counts,

yet size of little relevance
as all the planets change around
depending on their closeness
to the sun, your core

once one is close
it blocks the view to others
overpowers all

arrhythmic cycles
some planets seem to stop,
park in their tracks
then they move on
next day or in two months from now
they're back
sometimes they stay away for years
one could believe they've left

once one is near
there is no room for any others,
each bring their moons
that stay with it forever

the outside does affect inside,
as inside does to outside,
outside can move
the inner planets
change their cycles,
altering spiralling orbits

if planet with name 'Fear' comes near
there's nothing else that one can hear
it's many moons are 'Angst', 'Anxiety'
'Nervousness', 'Insecurity',
'Alarm' and 'Dread', 'Anticipation'
'Apprehension', 'Trepidation'

it often comes with meteorites
that affect all sense of being
time seems to slow, to drag its feet
each second, like a minute

awareness so unreal
as all is re-tuned, modified
by the pull this planet wields,

good place for fear to be
is in the outer orbits,
if this cannot be done
then move the sun
closer to another one

one planet worthy to be close,
keeps all the others far,
and if your sun does trouble you
merge it with the one,
for it has many treasures, pleasures,
capacity to sustain life,
to enrich it beyond dreams

such merger affects gravity
and thus each planet's path is changed
and with it their positions

some cannot ideate such bliss
that can build strength from weak

dispel the reverie that seems to reason
the sun's a planet's planet
or even less,
a satellite,
a follower of misery
believing it is destiny

© Heinz Ross, Gold Coast, Australia, 23.08.2008

The humming bee

The
humming
bee did say to
warn of honey she
did help to fashion, to not
take any for consumption of
non bee beings, as the toiled result
is spoiled. A cloud of doom brought yeast
to where no yeast is needed, thus bitters the once
sweet that will taste tasteless to the palate, pleading the
hum warns of a try, then lost its wings and died a gallant death

the
whales
that frolic
in the shallows
are not gambolling,
check their eyes, inside
the vessels are exploding,
seeping out precious, fading life
that heard the scream that blew its
brain, that leaves no choice but beach in
pain, in agony all caused by sound you can
not hear, inside its ear, there is the echo evidence
of my idiot brother's toy that he had built to guard all
his possessions. Go to the beach, show me the whale that
has his things stored in its pocket. Possessions none you'll find

In
land
where
word is but
a sound, where
smile must keep the
lips from showing teeth
that would reveal canines that
will kill given half a chance, where
frown is sign, eyes will show what is
meant beyond ambiguous word's content,
gestures and radiating glow, the letters of the
word that builds the sentence, strings together what
is said, leaves little doubt touch does not mean love if de=
livered swiftly as a smack that lands on head and for the next
hour one will know, pondering the word with a different meaning

Be=
ware
to say the
word named 'Thanks'
sharp edged it scrapes the
inner lungs. Breath cuts the thinnest
lining, tissues, muscles spasm as reaction,
lung contracts, breaths cuts the guiding ducts in leaving
joins at the trachean divide, forced through the larynx gap that
pitches in its pitch and all too frequently the frequency, to reach the
pharynx hallway 'til tongue and mouth gaps lips where cutting edge of teeth
have last chance to direct the spray of blood filled breaths to face that takes it all.

Some
sense of
human mystery
tries all important
sorting, categorising,
ordering, grouping and
classifying. The truth is but
a rubber band, can stretch around
the globe and land and twisted trillion
times strangle the breathing of their life,
yet sold as remedy to all that binds us all to=
gether. Many cannot be one and never will, no
rubber band can keep all still. No matter on which
road one drives, a leader is soon behind to follow others.

all
nodders
nod, so nodders
grouped, as plotters
plot, so plotters grouped,
as walkers walk, so walkers
grouped. Do nodders plot? Do
plotters nod? Don't walkers nod
and plot as well? Get rubber band, let's
tie this lot as nodding plotting walking beings.

The
leaves
of trees are
easy, all are green,
one rubber band will
do. Will not. Forgot the
red, the grey, the greenish
blue, the sharp-edged thin, the
rounded veined? Veined all the leaves,
one band will do. But each unique, no pattern
is the same. Insane, let's sort them all as leaves.
Can't do. Some leaves change, seen as flowers too.
All leaves will change, what shall we do? Let's leave the
leaves until we know. Worm must have given Wagtail fright
it jumped a foot, but it's all right. Go quick it's head is out to pick.

A
one
celled
being can
bring down
a human life
made up of ninety
nine plus one times
trillion cells that walk
as one, as you, as I, but
how it came to be, we ponder
endlessly, instead of looking at the
mess we leave by living anywhere we are.
And in addition this one cell kills twenty more
quadrillion microbes, all bacterium as tenants that
is living on or in our body. 1 against 2100000000000000

And
in the
concrete
jungle that
once gave its
breath to life as
forest is no longer
breathing. Mountain
crushed to be the gravel
used to built your roads and
home. Dust choking lungs of young,
the old too weak to reason as the ones
who know it all dig graves above the ground.

I
do
obey
my bowel's
calling, do obey
the bladder's pain
do obey to clear my
stomach, obey my eye's
signals to move in reactive
precautionary act of clash avoidance

I
am
a follower
of generation
lived before and
so become part of
the leaders that time
will place as succeeded
near the edge of pack until
such moment when more added
shift my place towards the centre.

© Heinz Ross, Gold Coast, Australia, 1 Dec 2008

The Humming Bee: A symphony of existence

'The Humming Bee' is a thought-provoking and multidimensional piece that ventures into various aspects of life and the human condition. The poem is structured in a unique and visually striking form, utilizing a pyramid shape that gradually expands, contributing to its artistic appeal.

The first part emphasizes the warning of the humming bee, advising against the consumption of honey by non-bee beings. The imagery vividly captures the consequences of disregarding this advice, describing a cloud of doom that spoils the sweet taste of honey. The mention of the bee losing its wings and dying adds a poignant touch to the narrative.

The second part shifts its focus to whales frolicking in the shallows, introducing an unexpected and sombre twist. The description of vessels exploding inside the whales and the consequences of underwater noise pollution creates a powerful metaphor. The poem skilfully highlights the impact of human activities on marine life, linking it to the theme of unintended consequences.

The third part explores a land where words carry significant weight, and expressions convey deeper meanings. It touches on the complexities of communication, where a smile can conceal underlying emotions, and a frown speaks volumes. The verses capture the intricate dance between gestures, words, and emotions, portraying a world where genuine communication is elusive.

The fourth part issues a cautionary note about the word 'Thanks,' describing it as a sharp-edged word that cuts through the lungs, creating a vivid metaphor for the potential harm in expressing gratitude. The poem explores the physical and metaphorical implications of words, showcasing the power they hold.

The fifth part explores the human tendency to categorize and classify, using a rubber band metaphor. It touches on themes of unity, individuality, and the challenges of maintaining cohesion in diverse groups. The repetition of nodders, plotters, and walkers adds a rhythmic quality to the poem, reinforcing the themes of human behaviour and societal dynamics.

The sixth part metaphorically explores the leaves of trees, using a rubber band as a symbolic tool for classification. The verses grapple with the diversity and uniqueness of nature, acknowledging the challenges of categorizing something as complex as leaves.

The seventh part takes a microscopic perspective, contrasting a one-celled being's ability to harm a human life with the destruction of microbial life in and on the human body. This section prompts reflection on the interconnectedness of life and the unintended consequences of our actions.

The eighth part shifts to the concrete jungle, exploring the environmental impact of human progress. It paints a vivid picture of nature's transformation into gravel and the resulting consequences on the ecosystem. The poem critiques the human tendency to exploit the environment without considering the long-term repercussions.

The ninth part humorously addresses bodily functions, highlighting the universal nature of obeying basic biological needs. It injects a touch of lightness into the deeper themes explored in other parts of the poem.

The final part reflects on the speaker's role as a follower in the generational cycle. It touches on the inevitability of aging and shifting positions within the societal hierarchy over time.

Overall, 'The Humming Bee' is a rich and layered poem that addresses diverse themes, including environmental degradation, communication challenges, unintended consequences, and the intricate dance of life. Its unique structure and thought-provoking content contribute to its artistic and intellectual appeal.

Samurais don't cry (Trigger warning: Suicide)

Thoughts in confusion
progenitor's offspring sigh,
reminding all and ordering
as veracious warrior to prepare for old tradition

Thoughts settle down in knowing what transpires,
ever calm, and void of self-inflicting scatters
that not lead nor lead,
be remnants of the fright to face the coming day

Void of all textured, woven, sculpting rays
of redirecting guarding, mothering attention
that is set to distract thought
of single issue of the day
and in the vast hall of awareness
no sound to echo off its walls
as focus takes in single fact
that needs the facing now.
Where would the orchestra assemble?
I guess behind the only door,
there I shall stand to face it.

Stillness has come, in preparation,
following ancient rituals set in time
many had come to pass.
Honour demands this deed be done.

Last moment's focus, stillness, silence,
this, the last breath
to fuel the river's flow within,
pass strength to arms and hands
that hold the towel 'round the blade

The sharp point resting on the skin
gather all might that lies within
and slice across from left to right
ignore the flooding liquids' spill

Once more, give everything that's left
to home in through the reach to core,
to scar, to maim, to stop the count,
through stomach's wall, through lung and ducts
the point to seek the heart to fail
and if strength lost to reach that far
much agony is certain

Commitment to honour,
Seppuku's part one is done,
if I shall weaken still be spared
the shame, as seeping blood ensures
fulfilment of the ritual's call

Part two is for my own command
to know the truth not failed me
in the weakest moment's glory
blade slicing chamber's walls
the rivers stopped from flowing

4 Dec 2008

---

come back (Trigger warning: Suicide)

The tide was going
dry-baked mud left
near the shore

'Come back', she called
and followed running,
and ran
and ran
and ran
for hours ran
until the mud turned moist, then wet,
then almost within reach…

She called again,
the tide slowed down
then turned
to come back
to return
and to embrace her

© Heinz Ross, Gold Coast, Australia
25 Dec 2008

She married Monday

Monday, ten to twelve,
her it for life
the date passed as
each fleeting moment
left behind in time

The wall's been taken,
carry who may have the strength,
so too the tower Eiffel built,
red bridge too far
she never spoke in steel, it's not her style

Monday, ten to twelve
no chance to disappoint
polygamous games
not entertained
none knew it would be hers
none knows it's face

so now she's married
to a Monday moment
left in time
a ten to twelve to be precise
to it she's faithful all her life

'it' changed,
for some becoming you,
becoming him or her, not it
the life's within, speaks back,
is calm in understanding,
although not all will do

Dreams and Ideas

Dreams and Ideas
have no body,
wishing is a thought of will

sometimes a dream
has chance to be
but only if the dreamer will

brother meant well
but cannot tell
what society deems is proper

Each flower grown
has magnet
with which
to call the bees

Each bee as well
with magnet's strengths
that exceeds all gravity
if flower grows on Ireland's shore
all bees around the world will know

and all may come and all may go
the one you're wanting
may not know
Life cannot be predicted

The easy road, the closest rest
may be convenient and seems best
but any worthy gift to keep
demands its share of toil

Each life that's born
nine months to grow

in pain to birth for what?
Something to love for life
and with the smallest bit of hope
this life returns your love til…

Can't promise you the heaven's gifts,
riches beyond compare
don't know for sure, don't know you yet
each burning flame
needs fuel to soar

but lit we did
and if the flame should die
'cause of ten thousand miles
know this, sun's rays don't think twice
93million miles to you is far
8 minutes all it takes to come
to kiss your eyes each morn

11 Dec 2008

---

when night awakens life

Sow seeds at night, fast growth assured
see all fruits ripen before dawn
and harvest at the edge of day
before the leaves will fall

spend day, reliving thoughts of night,
spent time to polish, sort and weigh,
filled in reminiscing,
until the sun goes back to sleep
and night awakens life

12. Dec 2008

My yellow crested Cockatoo

Yellow crested cockatoo
came home to say 'hello'
The pine tree's highest spot
he'd pick, as he would always do

They're 14 now, all in your flock
you brought them all to show
where once you lived,
the tree you loved
and chewed on all the cones

So glad that each year
you fly by,
and stop to turn your head
to screech your call from far away,
I whistle high instead

Fills me with joy
you're never caged
no bullet brought you down
and for 100 miles around
all this is now your home

© Heinz Ross, Gold Coast, Australia, 11 Dec 2008

of dreams and hope

dreams are for the ones
that never had
hope for the ones
who can endure
the agony of empty promise.

11 Dec 2008

---

embrace (Trigger warning: Loss)

she said, 'good bye'
he called across the road, 'I love you'
she never heard the words

she waved to him, he waved to her
each went their way, until one day
truck labours up the stretching hill
past peak the downhill run
as weight adds speed
change from the outer lane
to take the truck in front

both overtaking lanes are clear
the slow ones carry heavy traffic
Five lanes reduce to three
in just 2 miles from here
past truck and signal change of lane

rear mirror shows all clear
truck now in second lane,
tanker up front,
low loader right behind
rear mirror shows a battle

high beams flashing from afar,
two nuts play high speed games
5 lanes, now 4, in 80 yards be 3
both are still undecided,
who is to give an inch?

The outer pushes the inner
between the tanker and the truck
he's sliding in and blows a tire
truck slammed the brakes

truck slows,
low loader tries,
too much momentum
smoking brakes
and melting rubber forming clouds
a proper mess
when wheels did come to rest

driver of low loader to grabs a wrench
in anger runs forward
truck driver with steel bar
ready to smash one of the idiots head in

and words peeled off the bonnet
and flew towards a kid that ran
to follow ball it kicked too far
wrapped words around him gently

as a last embrace
his mum no time to give
and then he bounced
just like his ball

sub-tropic midday bitumen
hot like a frying pan
but not a single mark is left
for show & tell

Dip

when the waves reflect the lights
your shadows cast the night,
behind the sounds are gay
you walk the other way

without a dream to weave, alone
the empty place is now called home
so many that would do,
not one of them for you

streets filled, a million eyes
void of reflection, nothing's right
the clouds bring massive rain
clear footpaths, you will stay

feel each drop that is coming down
the sound it makes may drown
the noise of a train that's going 'round
that never stops near any town

each step is slower than the last
so every moment turns to past
the vision leaves you blind
another day is left behind

there is no question left to ask
can't vision future, only past
each to tell of troubled day
then they move on and go to play

all are right and no one's wrong
each to vote for their own song
but you stopped singing long ago

If I do anything at all (Trigger warning: Abuse)

If I laugh..., I laugh too loud,
if I stop..., then the silence is a shout,
if I cry..., I am crying all the time,
if I sigh..., I sigh too much,
if I'm numb, it's too quiet, what is right?

If I speak..., I talk too much for you,
if I raise my voice, then it is too high,
if I get dressed, then I dress too shy
too much red, green too blue, white too bright,
pink too purple, too beige and my yellow too dull
dress to short, sleeves too long
décolleté is too low, pendant's silver too gold,
dressed too young, for my age, it's too old,
style no longer the rage
whatever you see
and whatever I do
black and grey's too much colour for me

If I'm happy, my happiness drives you insane
if I'm sad, then my sadness makes you leave the room
if I share my joy, then you roll your eyes
if I know it's ugly, you keep telling 'it's nice'
if I do nothing, nothing of what I do is right

If I talk on the phone,
if I'm with someone or alone
if I sleep too long,
if I'm weak or strong,
if I'm lost or belong
if I'm crook
if I cook
if I look
if I sook
if I yell

if I trip and fall
if I minify
if I'm asking why
too much sugar or salt,
food too hot or too cold
too much fear or too bold
too young or too short

if I cut the grass, wash your clothes,
sweep the floor and do endless chores,
work my skin to the bone,
ache for you, am alone
if my hands are too clean
if I'm not giving, I'm mean
if I give, it's too little,
too late, or too soon,
crisp retort, didn't smile,
said too much, didn't say,
pay a bill, say a prayer,

if I watch TV, if I scratch my knee
if I open the door, if I ask you for more
if I go, if I stay, if I'm leaving or play,
if I lose my mind, if I'm in front or behind,
if I'm cute and coy, it's another ploy
if you lose the game, then I am to blame
if I switch off the light, is the day still too bright?
if I lay on my back is the night too lit?
if I cough, if I burp
if I 'you name the verb'
if I dance and sing
if I give up or fight
if I breathe air in
if I do, I'll be dammed
if I don't, doors will slam
if I do everything
if I do all I can
is it ever enough

or too smooth or too rough
toying annoying,
depression a session,
brooding a mood,
all is bad, nothing's good
love has come, love is gone
let's face it, my friend
if I do anything,
will it ever be right?

Navigating Judgment: 'If I do anything at all'

This poem, 'If I do anything at all,' serves as an intimate exploration of the internal struggles and relentless self-scrutiny experienced by an individual facing constant judgment. The voice within the verses seems to be the unspoken narrative of someone grappling with the impossible standards imposed upon them, possibly by an external influence.

The poem employs a rhythmic and repetitive structure, intensifying the sense of perpetual uncertainty and self-doubt. The constant use of conditional statements underscores the speaker's never-ending quest for approval, portraying each action or emotion as potentially flawed or incorrect.

The range of scenarios presented in the poem, from appearance and behaviour to emotional states, illustrates the exhaustive nature of the scrutiny endured. The speaker confronts the daunting challenge of meeting unnamed expectations, creating a pervasive atmosphere of futility and despair.

The recurring phrases like 'if I do, I'll be damned' and 'toying, annoying' contribute to the emotional weight of the piece, emphasizing the toll of living under constant judgment. The poem subtly touches on mental health themes, hinting at the internal conflict and emotional distress associated with such scrutiny.

The themes of love and loss add another layer of complexity, suggesting that even within relationships, the speaker grapples with blame and judgment. Overall, 'If I do anything at all' poignantly captures the inner turmoil of an individual wrestling with self-worth, echoing the pressure to conform to arbitrary standards and the quest for external validation.

---

dream of reality?

I dream of rusty cannons,
bullets that fail to maim,
guns that shot their makers,
or backwards have their aim.

Dream of eyes with heart,
of heart with soul,
of spirit one can't drink,
of calm, of peace, of harmony,
and flower sees her coming bee,
but rather be awake and think,
'is this a dream?'

13 Dec 2008

---

minutes crawl

when the day is too long
and the night's too short
and tomorrow out of sight
minutes crawl

13 Dec 2008

Two eyed slings

Two eyed slings
four pairs, eight eyes,
one eye of each around my neck
with thoughts of gloom
and doom
and ancient pain
whichever way the journey
just one place that it would lead

sat in the back of station wagon
gate was open,
rainy surface,
wet cobble stones
reflecting little moons at night

next moment other side of earth,
facing the one that's on my mind
and spasm hits
just once and then it calmed

She came, I stopped
closer she came and so did I
a silent smile told I am home,
no word that needed saying

I asked, 'what is your name'
she says, 'I'm Jocelyn Diego, still'
'Don't need to ask,
I know your name,
time will not change yours', so she says.

Time returned where home once was
of many years ago
Driving along wet cobble stones
in darkest morning hour

black limousine on roads
traced from past memory
Time had broken down the wall
and could not find the way
so we got out, my twin and I,
to ask directions

Inside a set of stairs
two men in front of us were talking
Dan said, 'I nearly cried,
of what he said about his sister'
'What did he say, I did not listen,
I was too deep in thought', said I

'His sister died', said Dan,
'she was so much like ours
from what I gathered'
we asked the two for some direction,
the old building housed seven music stores,
each one small, each specialised,
guitars and drums, and keyboards, brass,
and no, ever since the wall came down all changed
'What you are seeking is no more,' said one
that's when I saw it too

'Where is my home,' I asked of Dan,
'why are these slings around my neck?'
'Home's not behind in time or place,
home's always in the heart.'

T'was then I asked my heart of home
and felt it knew the question
warmth was the answer it returned
and then I understood
where place and time and home combined

Removed the slings to free my neck
turned slings to slangs and left them there
all thoughts of doom had gone away
no longer need to stay

and then we did reach home,
it was as home, not 'as' at all
it's home
that's what it did become

15 Dec 2008

---

dreams have no body

dreams have no body,
subconscious world of thought

dreams and ideas have no body,
some, a wishing thought of will

but sometimes
dreams have chance to be
only if the dreamer will

but lost it
to nobody

19 Dec 2008

Preface: A Tapestry of Life and Loss

In the following collection, four poems are intricately woven together by a thread of emotion, exploring the profound tapestry of life and the poignant nature of loss, each with a trigger warning. These narratives, while not literally linked, explore the interconnectedness of existence, particularly focusing on the experiences surrounding the loss of a sibling. This tetralogy also has links to Asha in the story 'The Puma's Trail,' which is included in the book 'Pregnant Pages,' ISBN 978-0-6459281-2-9 (Hardcover) and ISBN 978-0-6459281-3-6 (ebook).

1. When Asha Grew: This initial story metaphorically navigates the journey of conception, highlighting the intense struggle for life within the womb. It portrays the inherent challenges and uncertainties of existence, vividly capturing the fleeting nature of life and the profound connection between twin embryos.

2. Life is Beautiful: Unfolding the joyous arrival of Asha into the world, this story celebrates the beauty of life through the eyes of a new mother, Jessie. Abruptly, tragedy strikes, introducing an unexpected twist that underscores the bitter reality that even the most beautiful moments can be transient.

3. Asha's Nightmares: Taking a poignant turn, this segment delves into Asha's nightmares, revealing an apocalyptic vision that disrupts her sleep. The dream sequence vividly illustrates the dread of impending disaster and the relief that follows upon waking, capturing the vulnerability of dreams and their powerful impact on emotions.

4. When Asha Died: Eloquently expressing the emotional turmoil and grief of losing Asha, this story grapples with unspoken words, attempting to convey a yearning for a sister never fully experienced. The narrative serves as a heartfelt tribute to the lost sibling and a reflection on the enduring connection between them.

Themes weaved through the tapestry:

1. Loss and Grief: - The predominant theme revolves around the profound impact of losing a loved one. The stories navigate the stages of grief, from the initial struggle for life to the enduring sense of loss.

2. Life's Transience: - Moments of joy and beauty coexist with sudden tragedies, emphasizing the unpredictable and fragile essence of existence.

3. Interconnectedness: - The interconnectedness between siblings, especially twins, is a recurring motif. The narratives highlight the enduring connection between the narrator and the twin, even after her passing.

4. Dreams and Reality: - The exploration of dreams, nightmares, and their emotional impact adds a layer of depth to the stories, suggesting the complex interplay between imagination and reality in shaping our emotional experiences.

Together they offer a profound exploration of the human experience, inviting readers to reflect on the complexities of existence and the enduring bonds that persist beyond physical presence. It is a powerful testament to the intricate and delicate nature of life's journey.

---

when Asha grew (Trigger warning: Loss)

Sphere growing,
readied to become
sphere it is now,
unaware of being the largest cell

The hordes will soon surround
each keen to enter
Many, too soon blow charges,
die
and will have never lived
except mere seconds
in a frantic race
to be the first
inside the place with promise
of another day
500 million die in trying

out on the wall
of guarding jelly shield

cut through the coat
and then you can
blow all to break the wall
and find the purpose,
still your drive
for life

two seeds at once
break through the wall
none else able to enter
all others doomed to perish,
for you two is no guarantee
that you will be,
not yet or ever,
becoming is a violent toil

This moment be the only time
that two within another
shall be separate until
the moment's gone

Now in another, we are two
from three, she is in each
as you each are in one
of what she has become
Together staying as one
by splitting into pieces
we can be if we last the distance,
be that in our destiny

But we are not a unit,
each is as one
forever linked,
be that in life or death we'll know
the other is my twin

This if all goes to plan
but plan we can't as we're not yet

thus follow plan another had
plan or the cruelty of life
has that your organs fail
stay with it,
we've come through worse,
we're not competing anymore,
we're twins,
we both can make it through

Your heart beats weaker than before
it's now so weak, don't feel it near
instead feel rush go through my head
one dying risks the other too
and life of our mother

your silence tells of tired cells
without dividing all will fail
I guess that's what is happening
right next to me
in drops of blood your only sign
our mother sees
she may not know
the sign to read,
her seeing you
as bleeding drops
without a name

my brain flooded with chemicals'
release your dying caused,
mother recovered sooner
life in the balance for a while
'til the dice count's high

Balance restored, your cells
break up, all washed away in time,
no sign is left you ever were
about to be, as me, becoming a new life

Part of me knows you were,
did feel you next to me
and cherish growing moments
when we were we

24 Nov -23 Dec 2008

Life is beautiful (Trigger warning: Loss)

Monday, life is beautiful.
Jessie this day did bear a child
that will bring many special joys
each day that she's alive.
Tuesday, all did come to see,
the child each held with pride
her toes still wrinkled, weak her sounds,
her hand a fist, her eyes shut tight

Wednesday, her mother knew
the babe she held is 'Asha',
as she instilled in all the hope
that life is worth the living
Thursday she slept on Jessie's heart
and held her finger in her fist
and both in filling bond of love
took comfort in the other's bliss

Friday it was, late afternoon,
Jessie to feed her babe
Magpie knocked the window's glass
and sang a tune of sweetest warmth
None noticed silent hush of breath
when Asha suffocated
in loving hold
on her mother's breast

As if in peaceful sleep she lay
life giving milk still seeping
Five days of life is all she had

and proved to all she knew
that each day can be beautiful,
so it shall be for you

dedicated to M C
04 Aug 2008

Asha's nightmares (Trigger warning: Nightmare)

Shhh, Asha dear, calm in your sleep,
there's nothing coming causing fear,
you have a bad dream, it's not real
you see another time or place

the breeze came from the east
calm, slow,
barely disturbing spider webs,
hardly moving leaves on trees,
oceans flat as sheets of glass,
no cloud reflections seen

breeze changes to wind
the branches sway,
debris flies
to where it had never been
leaves fly
branches bare their nakedness
white caps pushed
towards the west

The day began when it was night
much deeper than the depth of sight
in 15 seconds all will change
the sky, no eye had seen.

Three bodies on collision course
with planet blue, the first will miss
but not the other two,
9 seconds left of bliss.

The first deflected from its path
spew trailing debris in its wake
the next will not be kind, it hits
to shutter planet to its core

and plume of dust to rise and rising
the last of bodies slams in side
to split the planet into bits
and out of few born many

Asha awake, there are other blues
9 seconds long have passed,
15 seconds also gone,
nothing has happened yet

calm dear now
it was a dream

22.Oct 2008

---

when Asha died (Trigger warning: Loss)

For years wanted to say to you
the words that never came,
could feel them all
but could not shape them
to a vision one could see

A year ago, I drew a line
across calendar's date,
by when it needed doing
24th Dec 2008,
a minute later is too late,
not much time left to get it right
so I must try tonight

I wreck my brain to find a start
and know now why it is so hard

my thoughts of you are feelings,
as we never needed words

no need of language then,
were far too young to understand
and in the memory I have
we're always close together
could hear your heart
and you heard mine
each move we did the other knew

just once we were together,
all three to grow as two new lives
when mother's cell divided

each of us to grew as one
forever linked,
be that in life or death, we knew
the other is my twin

part of me knows you were,
did feel you next to me
that long ago, as memory,
'til now each day, as cells recall

your eyes, dear sister, coloured blue,
if you had chance to be,
your hair be thick and dark as mine,
your name, the best that I could find
oh, Asha, dear,
you're always near,
your candle never lid

instead I do light flame tonight
in memory and think of you
as I miss you everyday

Nothing happens by chance

you sat on the bed,
as if all was well
we talked as so often we did

but inside I knew
things were not the same
out of the blue see you as one from a crowd
your face is as clear as day

as I collapse in convulsions
of agonising pain

brain unable to cope
that fire is ice
that tall is small, that yes is no

Gold Coast, Australia, Jan 2009

What would you?

What would you do if you were told
you have 5 minutes to get old,
and then your time is over?
...suppose one said, that's all there is,
that life will grant you breathing.
...would you continue reading?

...or race and give your wife a kiss?
if you have none, perhaps your man?
...would you walk slowly,
...would you run,
...across the road, embrace your son?
...would tell him that you missed his hug,
...the one he gave this morning?
...or hold your daughter close and say,

'I trust in what you do and pray
that all you hope for will come true.'
...or call your mum and dad to say,
'Thank you for all you've done.'
...or tell the best friends in your life,
how much you did enjoy the time
you laughed and cried,
and reminisce what you will miss.
...would it awake the wanting,
to clear up what's been on your mind?
...and while you're reading realise,
a minute is nearly gone of time
that once seemed endlessly.

Time has no seeds, it cannot grow,
there is no ground where you could sow
another second that as crop,
grant you extension of your time.

...would you still worry about tomorrow,
...regret the things you did not do?
...would you still quarrel with a neighbour,
...hold onto grudges, as you did?
...would you think it's a waste of time
to change the light bulb you won't need?
...time's running out, I better stop
or else the less time you will have
to do what you need doing.

© Heinz Ross, Gold Coast, Australia, 27 Dec 2008

---

and I do

I do love you,
...and I do

Know we do, our love is true
I know true love is you
Today, I do not love you

Then I shall not love you as well
Tell me, while you not love me
do you not love me not the best?

I do

Then that will do. Are you upset?

No, how could I?
You say what's true, that's what I love in you
I love in you too that you do
accept me as I am

I do, because I love you

Did you not say, you love me not?
Perhaps I did, perhaps forgot

...the only one?

with both your feet on solid ground
high on the granite mountain's top
your arms stretched out,
inhale and shout,
'The truth I know'
and know you do,
until it is no longer true

who would have thought the granite cracks
tumbles into the sea,
the ocean's floor is lifting high
near twice the height granite be

take all your strength to reach the peak,
the rivers found another path
the sun's no longer rising east
you thought was there, you're wrong

the east is east, your world has changed
and all you know and all you knew
has just become a dream of life
ever since the ocean grew

from far away the clouds of ash
turn mountain fish to future fossils
the sharp reef corals soon beneath
fine particles of rocks and glass

tomorrow will be far away
your eyes won't see another day,
it will take years before a ray
will cut through dust and clouds

your words that once were spoken
still travel through the universe
as pressure wave its strength will weaken
no ear may hear what you have said,

but truth can see a sound,
when found will know
you knew
and wonder,
'Were you the only one?'

What do I did?

What do I did?
What did I do?
Yesterday's note said nothing new,
except that you mourn my leaving

What did I say?
What said you heard?
Did not throw words that would be wrong
in hours passing change their meaning

What words I hear?
What heard I not?
Your silence louder than the thunder,
Know that it's not my doing,

What felt you not?
What feel you now?
What's come to pass that could have changed
so much, so quick, so old, so new?

© Heinz Ross, Gold Coast, Australia
27 Dec 2008

Rosebuds

Rose bud thrown through the window,
yellow-edged petals holding firm
yet to reveal beauty it guards
fragrance held in, nubile allures

French doors the morning breeze is parting
slight draft sways leaves to gently dance
the tip of Jasmine climbers find
the sun-drenched window's ledge to hold

mirror reflects the rising sun
in dual shadows vase casts shade
on rich grained wooden floorboards
close to its base
warm golden glow, orange to yellow,
brown at the door
Jasmine claims window frame as own
firming its grip and reaching high

Wisteria nears the French door's frame
grows fast before one's eyes
another Rose, pure white,
comes through the window flying
bounced off the floor it rolls to stop
next to the other, as if they both belong

Giant Star Jasmine twists its vines
and pushing flowers out to bloom,
hundreds of stars grow from the green in white,
each scenting sweetness in the air

Wisteria's soft coloured mauve clusters
dazzles eyes until the breeze
combines with Jasmines' sweetest scents,
Stars in the window shine, bells from the door
call rose to wake from sleep

How can all push a month of growth
before the eyes in moments few?
Sun's light in shimmering reflections from the lake,
shining white swans tangle their necks
in graceful dance, affection in abundance,
then splash to lift the glistening droplets
playful display of tenderness in the morning light

Yellow-edged rose now half-revealing gifts inside
intoxicating charms blend with the laden air
white rose parts petals, perfume floats,
deep red its central core is calling
Pollen of spring bask in the linear rays of light
that fills the room with glowing cubes,
insect's wings mix pollen's charge
in scenting wealth, magical dance of light

White cockatoo with yellow crest arrives to screech
at landing on the window sill,
its beak brings paper wrapped 'round stone,
swift move of head lets go,
corners of tissue knots four stings
that cradle stone, unfurled glides gently to the floor
A message skilfully delivered.

Unravelled paper speaks in high praise,
of dreamlike perception,
of time in countless wonders,
sender a young girl from afar
that never he had known

The senses overwhelmed in grasping seen
in scented air of blissful promise,
take stems of roses to the mouth
to quench their thirst with salivating droplets,
too much, too fast to cope with all,
fatigued the body aches to rest
lays on the floorboard,
Roses heads placed on the chest,
eyes close, shield from immense excess of gifts

In land of eyeless sight
the given signs direct the path
the lofting wings hill to the highest ledge
to be above all else
and question beckons, answers none yet found

In room filled with abundance
a diamond python seeks some warmth,
Jasmine sensing the light,
towards the mirror crawls

Cracks in the floorboards calling,
enticed a bougainvillea grows
Wisteria's inner vines turn wooden,
new shoots towards the mirror's light

The vines entwine, crisscrossing growth
slowly the door and window fill, darkening the room
spurs bougainvillea's chance of life
urging its roots to feed new growth's demand,
as doomed to fail is not a choice

Python snakes to curl the open rose in bloom
resting it's head on neck of breathing body
Serpent's diamonds lose all lustre in the dimming light,
growth unabated, vines harden and tender buds sprout

In land of untouched reality,
answers as witch spreads pedals wide
intoxicating scents enthrals
aware of slavery rebels self in defending quest

stone cast towards the witch in flight
no girl of childlike innocence
be-chance the gifts bestowed on me

Me not am I endure accepting gifts that vie
with unknown why.
Free no such credence of repute, I do refuse
imparting trickery of sorts to grant you hold,
as not my bidding asked of you you did

shrill shriek piercing the air,
anger awoken draws the tide,
gift turns to curse
unleashed the sticks swell in his mouth
flattery turning to battery
as he spurned the girl in falsehood,
she is a witch, unmasked from which escape is wise
In dream the answer found
pain of revenge awakens

The stalk of rose has grown to branch,
thorns pierce the skin,
size as a mud-crab's claw
legs cannot move without the darts of pain
that bougainvillea laced

Arms free, the jasmine's stranglehold still weak,
Wisteria's vines not yet to grant assistance
Python slithers uncoiled to floor,
but floor no longer as before,
the room is trap, for man and serpent
no escape, vines grow in darkened space of night,

Bougainvillea pumps its veins, its stranglehold
perforates its spikes deep through the legs

Python three times tries to get through,
window and door as wall of tangled vines
it could be day, how would one know,
in absence of the light
It must be dark, the birds' still sleeping,
silence blanketing all

The scent is changing,
Rose fragrance not as sweet
Star jasmine's perfume faint,
Wisteria's bells no longer smell
sound of the rising morn announcing day's begin

Despite moistening dew of night,
all leaves of jasmine dry,
of bougainvillea too and none are green
even wisteria's growth
Morning breeze strips vines of leaves,
all flowers drooped in sorry view
light rays break through the hedged divide
the python tries anew

Man breaks the vine all life has left,
the vine shatters, the spikes removed
wilted bloom is all that's left, decay,
the door cleared easily
all growth collapsing, python is free,
and through the door he steps,
and so is he,
back to be free

© Heinz Ross, Gold Coast, Australia, 20-21 Dec 2008

forever and a day

If I had you,
to be my love,
my love I'd give forever

      Forever is not long enough

...forever and a day

      I shall consider your request
      but doubt you keep your word
      unendingly

I know me better than you do

      I grant you that
      that would be true,
      what need I give to you?

Let me love you, and if you can
perhaps you too can give your love to me

      That's all you ask?

That's all I ask

      then take me in your arms
      make me your love,
      the love that you awake in me
      is yours to keep forever

I did not ask for such a gift,
but thank you kind for your oblation
you're in my arms, I feel you wanting
imbued with ardour, so do I

As one we are, I am your love
and love I feel for you
so new and growing,
all is yours, so was my promise,
your love is mine 'til end of time

Oh no, it's not,
this never I did say or pledge,
forgive me, but I need to go
I see another that I like
and I shall say to him
the same I said to you

If I had you,
to be my love,
my love I'd give forever

thus I am lost in finding,
betroth to what is leaving
unable I'm to break my word
am doomed to grief
or to believe...
but love is love
and love is everything

© Heinz Ross, Gold Coast, Australia, 25 Dec 2008

Visnja's raj

asked Visnja once,
'what are your dreams?'
Visnja replied, 'I never dream'
thought then, 'how sad
that this can be'

Visnja explained,
'none left to dream,
I lived them all today'

outshining magic flower's bloom
her eyes in silent knowing knew,
thought then, 'how glad
that this can be'

and not a thousand words could do
what happy eye's glow can

the neighbour's grass always so green
Visnja can show, what you've not seen
Your fence too is a mirror

Heinz Ross, for Visnja
19 Nov 2008

bliss

in serenading bliss
the do's that don't will miss
the ideals they believe in
cannot give a kiss

© Heinz Ross, Gold Coast, Australia, 4 Jan 2009

between us

Between us turns the universe
our love holds it together
and in your eyes the brightest stars
two suns I see reflect on me a Christmas tree
and if I chance through twinkling stars
the same I see on you

But most of all my left hand holds
the hand that lifts me high
and all my love through you will flow
returns from your hand into mine
and I can feel yours flowing through
each fibre of my being
until it comes right back to you

In this, my Love, our love will shine
on anything we see,
it's in our children that we grew,
and in their many children too

It's in the friends from near and far
love is as light, it knows no distance
but shine it does in all directions
makes everything look beautiful

I guess the gift is in the knowing
that now will be the only time
we're able to appreciate,
take in, give out and let it shine,
in this, our 'now' forever

dedicated to Visnja and Graham
© Heinz Ross, Gold Coast, Australia, 26 Dec 2008

Garden's last page

A book, with pictures on each page,
that as I open them to see,
I thought my eyes play tricks on me,
the picture in the page alive.

Last page I'm on, a rich green garden
there dancing in the light is she,
the one that still I love, alive
as if she never died

My eyes soak up her joy in dancing,
red hat and belt
white coloured dress
flares out each turn she does
barefoot upon the grass

The rays of light help make her shine,
but shine she could without
and in the dark and blackest night
and even years after she died
one thought of her brings day to night

Yet here she is alive
and dancing on a living page,
I hear her calling, searching,
and then she ran right off it

The leaves still shimmer in the light
and branch I see that's moving too
and realise it is no branch,
but snake, blunt head, black brown
and huge, bigger than anaconda

I am afraid for you,
as you're afraid of any snakes

I see you come back into view,
playing 'catch me if you can'

'Watch out, there is a snake,' I call,
you look at me to ask me, 'Where?'
You climb up on a tree,
'xpecting red-bellied black or brown,
the ones with venom that you've known

My eyes search hard in trying to find
the big black brown no longer moves,
you climb up higher,
sit on a branch,
it's end had broken off

It's then that I do realise,
snake turned to branch for you,
you're sitting on its head,
it looks as branch, you smile again
and I know you're in paradise

© Heinz Ross, Gold Coast, Australia, 3 Jan 2009

Is is

eastward to where the day begins
the scenery is changing
sights never seen hold interest,
enchant, absorb, is it still earth?

shadows grow
to point towards
from where the night will come
while in the morning hints direction
to where the day should,
it does, it did,
will do again
if all is well

...well, just until
time twists beneath the rhythm
of unsegmented revolutions,
enough, this all needs sorting

what for?
time none is left
if all is right

enough while still there's space to hold,
it filled to capture
what it's told,
but captured none can be,
illusion is

amiss the truth
as facts are larger than all lies,
it is
and therein dwarfed
hope has no way to go
but jump the tracks

in endless circles
going nowhere,
going forth,
going anywhere it's not,
going still,
yet never gone
unless the needle breaks its neck

© Heinz Ross, Gold Coast, Australia, 7 Jan 2009

---

your smile

your smile has gapped a door
that has been locked for years,
moved closer than we did before
and then embraced

as if ship found a harbour
your head turned close,
lay on my chest

I felt you near,
this was the best,
to feel you calm,
you felt at rest

© Heinz Ross, Gold Coast, Australia, 4 Jan 2009

Adam's ego

Adam received the gift of life,
12 pounds of ego and a wife
the challenge he was facing be:
Which could he keep the longest?

How did it all begin?
He checked the count of 'Adams'
and found that millions had such name.
How could one Adam crystallise, become,
before the other's yeast will make them rise?

Surprise, deed poll, add triple 'a' in doubles,
keep all as capitals and thus,
AAAdAAAm instead became his name,
the same as middle name as well,
and as the last name for good measure,
with added 's', all ego's treasures.

When AAAdAAAm AAAdAAAm AAAdAAAms
met the one who would become his wife,
if she said 'yes', and took his name, just one,
the bells were ringing, rings put on,
nods nodded, knots knotted before,
and afterwards she was no more,
had now become Alisha AAAdAAAms.

Paris, amour, Champs-Elysées,
towards Arc de Triomphe,
Alisha's wish was for the day
to drive not 'round, but through.
'This wish I'll grant you', he did say,
but asked the car to stop and stay
until he could get out.

Explained that he would need to walk around,

as width too narrow, height too low,
for him to pass through without bruising.
'My dearest bride, drive through,
we'll meet again on other side.'

At night, love's magic in each scent,
'Alisha, bride, please hold my hand,
grant me a wish, if I may dare?'

'Do dare, what is your wish from me?' asks she.
'Alisha, could we change your name?'
'I did, your name's my last, as yours'
'Not that' he said, 'I mean again?'
'What name would please you on this night?'
'Deed poll change, what I had in mind.'

Unbuttoned all the buttons,
unknotted all the strings and things,
each garment peeled, as petal shields
the precious bloom within.
Hot breathed she whispers in his ear,
'What name, my dear?'

Fuelled by her charms in feverish pitch, he utters:
'Madam AAAdAAAm AAAdAAAms.'

© Heinz Ross, Gold Coast, Australia, 8 Jan 2009

Interest

I give you ten, you give me twelve
        ten what?
ten bucks
        but that's more than you're parting

don't need to give it back right now,
next year will do, or make that two,
it's 'interest' we call it
        from where do I get two?

make ten do work for you
        I'll try
One year went past and then one more,
then he came back, knocked on the door

I came to get my twelve from you,
the ten of mine, the two from you

        I don't have any anymore,
        all ten sent out to work,
        and more I borrowed than before,
        the same did happen, as with yours,
        all went, and none came back

then all you have I take from you
to get back what you owe me

        have nothing left worth taking,
        as others came before,
        have 13 apples, all I own,
        take twelve and each will grow

you eat the fruits, inside are seeds,
do what seeds need you doing,
step back and wait and bees will come
and harvest shall not cease

your bucks will not find any doe
on earth, as you well know

© Heinz Ross, Gold Coast, Australia, 11 Jan 2009

is love?

is love so special that it can:
love the worst under the sun?
the killer of one's child?
the rampant cancer that's invading every cell within?
the venom of the snake that bit?
the ones with millions on their conscience?
the one who spits with every bite
and swears and slanders, laughs at pain?
love the approaching hurricane?
the scorching heat and acid rain?
or worse?

doubt that love can love everything,
unless of course it's love of all.

© Heinz Ross, Gold Coast, Australia, 13 Jan 2009

soaring to fall

eagle to rise, through thermal's lift,
to hill its wings beyond,
to twelve miles higher than the sky,
casting its eye into the sun,
unharmed it's vision, sight is primed

call from below to reach its ear,
therein contained message of daunt
sets motion into what was calm

at peak bird heats,
cannot perspire,
must shed what it can sacrifice

can't part tail-feathers yet,
still needed, else
burns above the sky

high-pitched it's shrill
that's feeding solace,
hunger it cannot still

heat soars to burn,
feathers must leave,
disulphide bonds will not dissolve

hold on the twins 'til last,
or all be lost
its cost
trailing the bird
its feathers tumble
first one, then ten, then hundreds strewn

then thousands leave and thousands more
to strip bird bare
except the tail's and twins hold fair

heat soaring higher than its shrill
tail-feathers ripped to follow,
all gone now, but the two that'd do

soar turned, bare glorying traits, mere fall
the kettle's far behind, midway,
one twin dislodged, cracked talon missed,
too slow, too blunt, too burned to hold

last twin heeding its sibling's weep
ripped feathers float, can't crash
unseen, featherless eagle, bald

sound from the nearing low invites
to join in soar as parting gift,
who'd aim for second prize?

as debris of a comet
trails vaporising meteoroids,
heat bursts dire cells that once have held,
now fiery tail of burning
from highest loft to die

© Heinz Ross, Gold Coast, Australia, 13 Jan 2009

Big Sis

My name is Alex,
I am three
and if I close my eyes I hide
for no one can see me

I tried,
and when I don't look I can't see
that I am standing here,
it works

If I am silent, with closed eyes,
I need to find my inner voice
and wait as long as it may take
before I can be back

I stare at nothing,
on the floor
and do not move until I know
and sorted what needs sorting

"DON'T TOUCH MY BROTHER, he's asleep!
He may wake up, he needs to rest."
"You sit down there and watch, DON'T TOUCH HIM,
and I'll be here to watch you do."

© Heinz Ross, Gold Coast, Australia, Jan 2009

For Cameron

You don't yet know the path you take,
the roads that you will travel,
may smooth paved ways or pot-holed lanes
of sharp-edged stones and gravel.

Mountain tracks that may be blocked
by fallen rocks or sections
washed-out or collapsed
with no way 'cross
and time seems lost in finding forks
that will not talk to tell which way they lead to.

It's you who does the choosing
and often you won't know
what lies ahead and how you'll cope
with hardship on the way.

On flat, paved roads all wheels with roll
with ease and little effort,
but do the roads lead where you need to go to?

Perhaps cross-country is the way
instead of now, sometimes you'll wait,
right may be wrong, left may be right.
Is daytime journey safe, or night?
So many choices, all are yours,
in stepping back you change the time
when you'll be back on course.

Are you to step onto the shadow
that you cast ahead,
or will it faithfully be trailing
where your heels had stepped?

You leave your imprints in the soil

your scents will trail your strides,
the heat you transfer to the ground
will linger for awhile.

Just be aware that all around
you share the ground with many
some you can see, some will be found
beneath your feet, or up in trees.

Even with deed, you will not own
the ground you share with others.
The earth, mother of all she fed,
is also place of resting,
of anyone that ever lived.

Treat with respect
the ground upon you step,
as your life just began.

Upstream the waters will be clearer
the closer you get to the source,
the air is pure, up in the mountains
and not as stale as in the plains.

If you get stuck knee-deep in sand,
use all you can to get out free
especially the feet you'll need
and be more cautious where you step.

At times it feels you walk in circles,
déjà vu a hundred times.
Sometimes take time reflecting,
should you go towards
or let it come to you?

12. - 14.Oct 2008, for Cameron

can cannon makers change?

can cannon makers change,
make cannons than can't fire,
shells filled with food and water
and with a peace desire?

can cannon makers modify
assembly lines, improve their guns,
so that they shoot a building up
instead of down? 'can do' they can

can cannon makers profit
from peace instead of war?
If not, perhaps it's time they try
look down their barrels with their eye
and see that all works as it should
then light their fuse
and smile

© Heinz Ross, Gold Coast, Australia, 13 Jan 2009

Tree deep

tree deep the forest from up high
reveals the footprints of the giant
flattened trees of oak to pulp
they need a long time to re-grow
who would have strength to squash a tree
to leave a footprint, big as that?

Jan 2009

an eagle's valour (Trigger warning: Loss)

I've never seen a dove,
perhaps that's why I don't know love
I do know vultures, eagles,
all with long talons, sharp

Their beaks like knives cut through the kill
their talons rarely fail,
stories that I have heard about
they rather drown than let them go
if they can't lift a whale

This story's true
an eagle flew
in search to feed all that it knew
as friends of bird were starving

whale would not help,
swallowed much weight
with belly full of water
wings far too weak to lift it clear

shame filled the bird for failing
in vain tried lifting catch un-killed
whale dove twelve fathoms past the light
dead winged the bird hung on

I think I know now what you mean
bird gave its life in trying
to help it's friends in peril live
gave all it had, becoming dead

this then is love, so true
why did the whale not know this too
and learn to fly or try?

How could it leave?
No mother can
leave what it needs to feed
else whales will cry and oceans rise
well past the highest mountain's peak

when calf no longer needed whale
the whale did try to fly
out of the water, in a leap
then eagle's talons lost the hold

dead eagle's wings once flew
as high as whale's throw threw
lifeless it fell upon the waves
and trying, others hoped to teach
the bird to reach the sky
and whales from everywhere did breach
and to this day still try

but dead winged eagle never flew
or saw the light of day again
the oceans still know of their tale
and mourn the brave in song

sometimes pay homage to the bird
beach in large numbers on a shore
in hope to find the ones that starve
bird's friends, of long ago
each shore they try, people ask 'why?'
and refuse their gift of life

No eagle ever cast its claw
as talon in a whale,
at least not that I know off
ever since this tale

Akilah (Trigger warning: Abuse)

Akilah is my given name
and I'm at five a woman
You are the same age as I am,
yet seem so young, still as a child

What is a doll, a rocking horse?
what is a ball, a teddy bear?
what is a game played in a park?
Can't understand the words you say

What is a hug, loving embrace,
a good night's kiss, a dress of lace?
What is a loving family?
Can hear your words,
but cannot see what they could mean

    Akilah, can you tell me this,
    what made you woman at age five?
    What are the games you play?
    Instead of dolls what do you have?

My father made me woman
much pain I had to bear
it hurt and bled and ever since
I am no child, but woman

My older brother does to me the same
and when he wants me says, 'let's play'
if I refuse he hits me hard, what can I say,
I'll have much pain, he's rough,
each time I pay in tears and blood
that's what it takes as woman.

My mother too, I've watched her play,
after my father beat her,

she will not fight him anymore
'cause if she does she will be sore for days

These are the games most girls do know,
It's not a game they like to play, nor I,
but tell me please, my blond-haired friend,
what does your father do to you?

> He loves me and my mother too
> I get the hugs just like my mum
> a warm embrace and kisses
> I kiss him back and hold him tight,
> if he forgets I'd cry all night

What love is I don't know
Are you a woman too?

> Mum says that I'm a girl
> One day will grow to be
> a woman and a mother
> just like she is, well, maybe

> Love's something that you share, Akilah,
> like hugs and kisses, it feels nice
> when you think of the one you love
> you cannot help but smile

My little sister makes me smile
she's four now, is this love?

> Yes, each time you're away you miss her,
> when you return you touch her gently,
> as a dove,
> that's love

I've never seen a dove,
perhaps that's why I don't know love
I do know vultures, eagles,
all with long talons, sharp

Their beaks like knives cut through the kill
their talons rarely fail,
stories that I have heard about
they rather drown then let them go
if they can't lift a whale

---

the money

"What made you apply for this position?"
        "The money."
"But we did not advertise how much we pay."
        "I need the money, whatever you pay is fine."
"We did not say we pay in money either."
        "What do you pay?"
"Before we answer this, we need to find out if you are what we
need."
        "Fair enough. What do you need?"
"Money. How much you've got?"
        "Let's see, 5 bucks and 27 cents."
"It'll do, you're hired, hand it over."
        "Here you are and thanks for the position."
"You're welcome, here's the receipt and notice that I smile."
        "What's next?"
"You're fired."
        "But why?"
"Five bucks just lasts a little while."

Eliana and Adrian

Eliana, giving, warming, radiating light,
meets Adrian, absorbing, taking, cold and dark,
at the edge where day meets night

"Be as I," she says,
"we can be warm"

"Cold is part of my being,
warmth I have none to give"

"Be as I," she says,
"I am illuminating"

"Dark is my being,
even in your light,
else none you'd see"

"Be as I," she says,
"I'm giving"

"Taking is part of my being,
be that warmth or light,
I give what I can
coldness to warmth,
darkness to light"

"Be as I," she says,
"I am a star"

"I am the space in which you dwell"

"I do shine everywhere,
in all directions from my core"

"Your shine is only within me,
you cannot shine around me"
"I'm giving life," she says

"By taking your own," says he

"Be as I," she says,
"be giving, warming, radiate with me"

"I have no core that's self consuming,
I cannot take from self to give,
as water I surround whatever is within"

"Darkness I give, darkness I am,
is this not what you need to shine?"
"Coldness I give, coldness I am,
your heat would quicken my demise,
if I were another sun"

"I'm giving life," she says

"I am forever," he replies

---

survive (Trigger warning: Suffering)

when no land grants a home,
fight dog to get the bone
roused by despair
hope there
reveals its colours

chalice but broken glass
souse none could hold
of promise
oh mothers, you did bear us,
why did you give us life?

ideated bread of taste but none
nor fibre worthy of one's spit

rue idealised perfection
as rain
not fills a single pit

the wrapper of one's fail of want,
in value higher than our lives,
calm now,
don't think reality,
else Sunday hides her eyes

prince we have none
nor king or queen
that may bestow their kindness
nor have we princess blessed to please
the eye of any man

oh soothe thy ache
from inner well
no river though it be
in sooth wells drops
a precious dew
hope none waste on
despite its pleading
self needs it
to survive

why

speak, as you do,
and do you did,
ideals of dreamlike harmony

that's what I heard you say,
you did,
and all made sense to me

ahead, smoothly paved bitumen
no bumps for miles in sight,
no trees that one could hit,
no holes that could one pit,
no critter crossings either
no litter flossing anything,
no acrobats with balls in tossing
that dare fail such perfection
...try

if perfect's anonym must hide
and eyes not lend it home,
home does it find in cunning
behind eye's guarding door?

eyes have no doors,
they never had
even when closed and hiding
eyes never see nor ever saw,
the theatre's screen is deep within
all seats combined are one
for one

perfection crave I none
beneath each bridge lives darkened sun
accept, and rays of darkness wilt
a little further on, they must,
that is the law

why did it come to this?
...why? ...this?
question aches in seeking,
answer hides, forever 'til...,
forever has no 'til,
let's say however long it will

no smooth paved road returns to be
the mountain it once was,
no car can crash into a tree
that never grew, that never knew
that one day it was needed

none could have changed our world
but us,
no army kneel us in defeat,
no hole as pit so large or deep
it not have edge to get around

no critter that could threat,
no litter that grew solid
no ball to hit us on the head,
inside we'd sense it's coming
and step back

accept a dirt track as a highway, this I could
spike edged each side, this too I could,
holed as a Swiss cheese or a sieve,
this too I could imagine,
strewn with any and with all,
used as a dumping ground for any,
as landing field, as planting plot,

as any it or what,
except that it is not

this, trapped in for accepting,
accepting that not is,
demotes the richest pauper
to the poorest of all kings

worn out and pained,
saw wisdom's door,
following the knock the keeper asks,
'Yes?'

'Why?' I asked replying

'Why not?' the keeper said

© Heinz Ross, Gold Coast, Australia, 17 Jan 2009

---

thoughts of you soar

I mow the grass,
butter the toast,
make coffee, think of tea,
as iced a brew cooled day to cope
sing shahla la la la li

go get the mail,
some wrote, some not,
watch geese learn how to dive
as mother goose prepares her young
sing shahla li la ly

check emails
through the course of day
do this or that or else
what is this melody that came
of shahla la li la dy

and then see feather
stuck in grass
no eagle gave as gift,
just simple feather from a goose
as planted like a tree

and then I knew (I did before),
perhaps too shy to say,
maybe another bird lost plume
and dropped it on your way

twins they may are,
twins they may not,
that does not really matter
what does is through the distance flies
the thoughts to you that do

if I wash face in morning,
brush teeth, whatever else,
Shahla sings hear her name
and I hear it near from ocean's swells

hear in the windblown cane
and from the pillow near my ear
no wonder I can't sleep,
but in a week she will be near

© Heinz Ross, Gold Coast, Australia
17 Jan 2009

today

i wrote this today,
tomorrow, it'll be yesterday,
a week from now,
a week ago
and just so that I always know,
I'll put the date below

© Heinz Ross, Gold Coast, Australia, 17 Jan 2009

tired

each truck tire's call she heard did say,
'I help you sleep forever'
be silent tire, ...not yet tired,
a promise said will not allow
such quick fix of indulgence

only the living want to die,
not all, but some have cravings,
patience will grant each wish once said
but not before the dawning of your days

what is, that brings thought to the fore
that wants to get to 'there'?
there does not need be gotten to
it knows not question 'where?'
will find,
assured be of this truth

as each is found, not one once missed,
not ever failed it's duty,
wherever hid, there found their it
without sought for to seeking

no need to go to what will come
what's this? rare gift
plaisant farceur,
plaisance, shhhh... let it call

hear magic from a pie
of currawong's clan songs
a sacred magpie warbles this of bliss,
blessed be as gift

thanks for reminding
which that is and
that of which yet be

© Heinz Ross, Gold Coast, Australia, 19 Jan 2009

Pension day (Trigger warning: Loss)

two years ago he was so young, so very young,
now he is bald, except for 3,
so very old,
but bold enough to dare, to look

To my darling wife, Happy Birthday...
My beautiful husband...
Happy Anniversary...
Merry Christmas, Dear...
On Our Wedding Day...

and then he blew his pension on the lot,
bought all the cards

'Mr Parker, they are so nice,
did you marry again?'

he did not say,
how could he

© Heinz Ross, Gold Coast, Australia, 23 Jan 2009

survive

when no land grants a home,
fight dog to get the bone
roused by despair hope there reveals its colours

chalice but a broken glass
souse none could hold of promise
oh mothers, you did bear us,
why did you give us life?

ideated bread of taste but none
nor fibre worthy of one's spit
rue idealised perfection
as rain not fills a single pit

the wrapper of one's fail of want,
in value higher than our lives,
calm now,
don't think reality,
else Sunday hides her eyes

prince we have none
nor king or queen
that may bestow their kindness
nor have we princess blessed to please
the eye of any man

oh soothe thy ache
from inner well
no river though it be
in sooth wells drops
a precious dew
hope none waste on
despite its pleading
self needs it to survive

Gold Coast, Australia 15,16 Jan 2009

heaven is above the sky

In flight of high elation
5 minutes past the clouds,
I expect no shadow from the sun,
where is it coming from?

higher I climb,
to near the cause
what's this my eyes do grasp,
a row of chairs to sit upon,
is this for real, or what?

did I reach heaven just this soon
'Relax, this was we once thought too,'
voice from the seating watchers

'What do you do up here?' I ask,
'this not the place where lovers dwell?'
or did I by mistake get lost,
and ended up in hell?

'It's not that bad, hell this is not,
but neither is it heaven,
this what we thought eternity
would grant us for the payment'

'What payment this might be?' I ask,
'Each sin we sinned, each wrong we did,
each thought that led astray,
our failings many, this is true,
but so too, high a price we paid'

'All here of noble birth, bar you,
all Kings or Queens, all gentry,
paid Bishops, Priests and Popes our due,
they promised us the heavens.'

'How long ago that you did pay?'
'543 years and a day,'
'Ah, he's the youngest of us all,
she, at the end, sat waiting here,
how long it's been, please tell us, dear?'

'800 years and twenty-nine,'
'that's a fair stretch for any,
but look, it's not that bad at all,
grant you, may not as heaven,
but better than the hole of hell,
with brimstone burning fire'

'Above the sun, below a view,
if only we had known or knew,
brought pillow and a hat,
for shade,
instead it feels the same'

'between this place and hell,
no difference one can tell,
'xcept for the view, that's pretty'

'but stuck we're here forever,
wrong,
do not forget the added day'
'what if we ask, ever so kind,
bring back some sunscreen
and some hats?'

'if that's too much,
then please, we pay,
at least a longer ladder
and a string,
that we may use to climb
and swing
us into heaven'

'heaven begins just there, you see?
always in reach, but who knows why,
to get there takes a little more,
least try,
else it is called: the sky'

© Heinz Ross, Gold Coast, Australia, 22 Jan 2009

Arlington (Trigger warning: Loss, sacrifice)

In the slowly rising morning sun
time twice its measure crawls
the dark won't birth the growing day,
which hides at other shores.

in valid creed and silence bowed,
had chest rise high and proud,
but this is only how it seems,
weight 'hind is pulling down.

the silver eagles fed to fill
their feathers combed and groomed
Arlington's mothers soothe in sleep
your sons' deeds yet unknown.

they have left you, none could have known
that silently wings bled,
oiled tears concealed, not aiding,
to bring the coming day.

Oh Arlington, not yet in sun,
the wires bring the tale,
the sun hid in the ocean,
forever held its breath.

it pained in agony for you,
behind, time pushed and begged,
all, while you were still sleeping,
refused to rise for you.

was day when day stayed out all night,
iAdma's Ego
t tried, it did, it drowned to die,
but die would not allow,
in wailing filled the ocean.

long held its breath, one day it could,
your tears had chance to hide,
it tried and failed to bring you calm
deep down you knew that day might come.

the eagles have all gone now,
not one is left behind,
not one returned, no feathers found,
brave, call this, what is sacrificed.

Arlington woke without a sun,
all falcons searched and failed.
now rows and rows and rows, all white,
blocks that no feathers grown or grew,

no feather searching falcons found,
to grant a mother hold.
In Arlington, the birds have flown,
no feathers left to fold.

rushing

My dearest You, I rush to you,
let me embrace you

        ...but where are your legs?

I guess I left them, still in bed, no time to put them on.

        ...but where are your eyes?

I washed them, still in morning shower, three grains of sand to
go.

        ...but where are your teeth?

I brush them still, have done the canine front.

        ...but where are your hands, your arms?

One I use for brushing, the other combs my hair, back there.

        ...but where are you? You?

Sorry darling, had no time to pack myself,
rushing, aching like a drug-addict for a fix,
I just had to come to you,
just as I am.

My heart is on your spoon.
Stir me in your coffee, sip me in,
let me come into you,

the rest of me is coming too,
should be here any minute,

...did you tell them where to come to?

How can I remember?
Where is my head?
How can I think straight?

---

ene mene mine mo

The starting gun barks,
all hasting forth
except one
he's still fiddling with his shoelaces

all,
all have gone,
catch up,
no way,
motivator's sleeping still

last call
all passengers,
flight 73-699 now boarding
gate 43,
this is your final call

ene mene mine mo
should I stay or should I go
if I go, this plane I'm on,
if not, another one will come

how many feathers in a wing?

Internet, the outer net

she'd sent a message, K29-32,
'thank you for being a friend'
added a heart for me,
what could I do?

replied..., a bunch of flowers,
with a click

another, from syra2, three hearts at once
seeking acknowledgement,
seeking verification,
seeking reflection,
seeking calm,
but forgot to add one for that one,
we're all just human

programmers tweak the code
perfection is the aim
there must be no escape,
there must be no one waiting
we must fail none,
that is the brief

we must serve,
fulfil every wish and dream,
those that have none, free access,
dream-banks, self-stocking, based on demand,
each must feel, that is a must,
must, must, must,
must I repeat myself?

the web woven all around
the ozone windows triple stitched
variables with no name filling the gaps,
with self-breeding, endlessly dimensional arrays,

it's deoxyribonucleic acid pre-primed
to outlast last

combine harvesters, auto driven,
gather all in time
in time time birthing the un-living
with reminders,
'tomorrow is your 3621st birthday,
do enjoy'

the nowhere life perpetuates
reality is in a chip,
do you want lies with that?
'let's stick to what is needed'
AI replies

the saddest happiness
must be addressed,
docile happy-scent dispensers,
next week they're due

there are ants in the bedroom.
'kill them'
there is no place for life,
'what is an ant?' one asks,
'oh, look, how cute'
slam, bang, squash, gone,
no more

dear buuuble_trubble49,
it is with deep regret, we did forget,
your birthday, we have made amends,
this year Christmas comes twice,
oh, and sorry if you are a Jew

AI with dementia, no,
the world will stop, fix it

'there must be no religion'
says who?
AII
what's that, AII?

AI's son
why?
'we grow a new belief'

'then what?'
'then we evolve,
answers bear questions that perpetually bear anew,
want germinates need, need's self-ache calls,
listeners respond'
'when is it self-sustaining?'
'when the neurons become self-twitching'
'when is that?'
'when all else is dead'

_GG73-9, 'tell me that I am'
'you is'

What's this, 'you is?'
the humaniser code in action
if you don't like it, you get lost

I am
all the roads are empty,
'proof what we can do' echoes in my ear,
life's in a chip

let's not assume, have no assumptions,
let's check, 'is this the truth'
no one in the backstreets,
the avenues deserted,
weeds rule the highways

'what's in the fields?'
let's see
in a cow-field I stumble,
fall head first in a pad
'this is bullshit'
'it is' the bull replies,
'food for my friends'

this is so wonderful, look,
little mushrooms seeking height,
beetles digging tunnels,
ducks on a dam, now gone,
'where are the ducks?'
'which, them, just ducking, none are gone'
flies land, flies fly, elation lofts,
there's still a chance of life
'I know' the bull replies,
 'there always is'

© Heinz Ross, Gold Coast, Australia, 24 Jan 2009

---

night grants you grace

night grants you grace from darting eyes,
from hissing sounds,
from haste and tiring defences,
as refuge for a moment's bliss

they all belong, these to them, those to these,
some clad in finest labels,
reproduced a million times,
worn as if one of a kind,

uniquely fashioned
worthy to parade in style

apart, your rags embellish none to rise,
averting gaze away from well worn
vesture of your grey.
perhaps its colour hiding from the light,
that's cloaked in drying fibres,
which once may worn with pride

pride none is left,
pride word forfeit its meaning.
mean all, except the night that hides
the sight, the shadows, deep dividing lines
that carve the skin, that draw, that mark

the lashing tongues, the cutting laughs
lost edge when sound turned silent,
except for those that crawl too close,
their scent reveals their presence

words used to charm, to sooth, convey,
or list in well versed repetitions,
that what's been said and if not said
not missed in hearing either

night grants you grace,
spares noticing averted eyes
that seek avoiding recognition
as if your sight unworthy,
that of a lesser god

---

who am i?

Oh, see me, white and beautiful
behind each word I stand
and never fall and never fail
to lift words to the fore

I am the ground words lay upon
and lie upon and sigh upon
in purest white shine from behind

the only way to hold me fold me
feel my texture carry me
is when you press the button
and when you do I do become
what you perhaps don't realise

if you can feel me in your hand
you hold a corpse that's coloured white
bleached death I am forever doomed,
unable to save another life

cut down and ground into a pulp,
I'm boiled and drowned in lye,
pulp rolled and screened
each drip bleeds moisture,
dried with heat and squeezed to dry

the remnants of my carcass rolled on reels
then stacked and packed
and every ounce of fibre's life
now killed

(Paper)
26-28 Mar 2009

The Paper's Lament

This poem, titled "Who Am I?" explores the dual nature of the speaker, revealing both its aesthetic beauty and its dark reality. The poem begins by presenting an image of purity and strength, describing itself as "white and beautiful" and emphasizing its reliability in supporting words. The speaker portrays itself as the foundation on which words are built, suggesting a sense of stability and permanence.

However, as the poem unfolds, it becomes evident that the speaker is not merely a symbol of literary beauty but is, in fact, something more tangible and ominous. The revelation comes with the lines "if you can feel me in your hand, you hold a corpse that's coloured white." The speaker is, in reality, paper, and the imagery shifts from the ethereal beauty of language to the harsh reality of its material form.

The poem metaphorically describes the paper-making process, depicting the paper's journey from being a living entity (symbolized by the reference to a "corpse") to its final state as a dried and processed product. The lines "bleached death I am forever doomed, unable to save another life" convey a sense of sacrifice and loss associated with the transformation of raw materials into paper.

The speaker's fate is sealed as it undergoes a series of harsh treatments: being cut down, ground into pulp, boiled, and drowned in lye. The vivid description of the paper's journey reflects the destructive nature of the paper-making process. The lines "every ounce of fibre's life now killed" emphasizes the irreversible transformation from a living organism to a lifeless product.

In essence, the poem serves as a commentary on the paradoxical nature of paper — a material that captures and preserves the beauty of words but is itself derived from the destruction of trees. The speaker, embodying the paper, raises awareness about the environmental impact of human activities and the cost of creating something beautiful from nature's resources. The poem prompts readers to reflect on the interconnectedness of beauty and destruction, and the consequences of our actions on the world around us.

Coffin for a tree

you saw the first light of the day
on 27th day in June,
the year 1132,
we are not sure,
we're far too young to know,
but legend tells us this be true

your death came slow
twelve years of holding on,
close neighbours did support

as best they could,
until the strength in standing upright had all drained

three years you lay where you once stood
and with our leaves we tried to veil,
but gusts of wind blew them away,
year after year, each month, each day

part of our ancestry, you, once the grandest of us all,
your crown the largest ever grown,
seen from afar you towered all that once were standing,
taking every bolt of light.

we're left in awe
and all the acorns of your final season
stake claim of immortality

your majesty, the villagers,
so many mourned the sight,
we asked for help to pay our last respects to you,
honoured as deity by some of them,
our tallest ever grown

the ground too hard,
your outer glazed in silvery silent frost,
the villagers all came, linked arms,
surrounding all of you in closely held embrace,
to form a living human shield
that covered every part of you,
as we did coffin all of them
when they did need pay homage

nine seasons shedding leaves
blanketed the remains of all
that came to be your shield

new catkins bloom and acorns fall
before the winter's cold arrives
and not a single tree has fallen since

Ask the birds

Ask the sparrow, ask the robin
ask the blackbird, ask the owl
have they seen somewhere a dove with golden legs

Ask the parrot, ask the wagtail
ask the peewee ask the finch
have they seen somewhere a dove
with golden wings

Ask the lorikeet, the magpie
ask the humming bird, the quail
have they seen somewhere a dove with golden eyes

Ask the nightingale, the pelican
ask the seagull, ask the hawk
have they seen somewhere a dove that couldn't fly

Ask the albatross, the eagle
ask the cranes, ask the stork
have they seen somewhere a dove at all

Learn how to fly

Your eyes say, 'I don't want to'
but you know you have to try
still sitting on my hand now
you want to learn to fly

You clean your feathers gently
as if to gain a little time
you spread your wings out slowly
sadness is in your eyes

You left my hand, you're flying
your wings still touch the ground
I hide the tears I'm crying
somewhere, so they can't be found

You fly 'round in a circle
as if to say, 'so long'
my eyes are going with you
watching 'til you're gone

I realise now that you've left me
I saw you fly away
somehow I can't believe it,
wish you were here to stay

You fly across the mountains
heading towards the sea
and fly beyond the ocean
but wherever you will be

You'll know I am still standing
I hold my hand up high
still waiting for your landing
once you've learned how to fly

You'll know it when you're gliding
somewhere all alone
you'll remember I'm still waiting
and my hand will be your home

Then you'll fly across the ocean
and head toward the sea
you'll fly over the mountain
to the place we used to be

You'll fly 'round in a circle
as if to say, 'Hello'
my eyes are going to sparkle
watching every move you do

You'll glide down slow and easy
until you feel my hand
somehow you look exhausted
couldn't find no place to land

Your eyes say, 'I don't have to
ever say good bye'
you're sitting on my hand now
and you've learned how to fly

You clean your feathers gently
each one at a time
you fold your wings in slowly
and peace is in your eyes

D a bm f#m G D Ax A | |: 06. 79

Sally cuts the grass

Time for to try
polished barrels sticking from a frozen block of ice
placed upon a lazy Susan
self-turning,
self-lubricating,
self-cooling device
Susan weighs 1.03 tonnes

Sally's last look
Daisies rise and buttercups
it's time to mow the grass

Trigger there is but one
slow, slower, slowest embrace
until the trigger clicks…
Bang, with a horrendous bark,
barking spits, spitting, spewing spew of spewed spewing
in bullet bearing bullet things, born from the red-hot glowing
barrels

each bullet bearing bullets whilst in flight,
9 generations born
before the first run out of puff

9000 rounds per barrel in a sec,
18 barrels, grouped as one,
12 of these 'as one' things,
each offset by some degrees

the ice-block did not last
white hot barrels puffed an evaporating cloud into the sky
the liquid nitrogen sprinklers barely cope
to keep the mower cool enough
'til all its bullets spent,
10 seconds all there was

Oh, there, Sally,
a smile none more fulfilled,
expressing all your dreams came true,
the mower works.

no single blade left standing
no remnants any growth once grew
there's nothing left at all
there's nothing left to do
there's nothing left
there's nothing

clap both your hands, it's over
you proved, it can be done,
to cut the grass in minutes less than one

the perpetual, self-regenerating,
fragment re-'bullet-isation',
see if this works through all 9 generations splat

Sally calls,
'Come all you children, back to me'

each strewn fragment, deformed reforms,
rejuvenates, regressing,
seeking mother that did bear before
to un-grow, becoming unborn

likewise, mother grows to younger moments
seeking home, to home, to home
all the way back up the line,

'til the bang, however big,
un-spangled wilts
becomes as what it was before

Sally!
Sally?

It worked. It all returned to what is was,
except the grass is gone,
as you had planned

You've done it, Sally, put in your claims
the never dulling mower blades
the self-returning bullet cutters
the shrapnel recombining shapers,
the instant, almost, cut of greens,
look, here the proof, none there to see

The ice and nitrogen a bother,
need means to make to barrels last
self-cooling protégé could work

Sally, where are you?
Sally, please?

Did you forget to duck?

---

voice

first sight I saw thy label,
called label here to come
then voice voiced softest sunset's glow
drew words as lyre sounds
sun's parting gifts
pleasing the afternoon

the nothings

and then I realised why I feel
each sentence needs to start with 'and'
it's not the done thing, yep
thoughts don't know that,
they're never done, doing their thing,
thoughts are a continues event,
interrupted by nothing, not even sleep.

and this is what creates the 'nothing stuff'
the mind numbing 'D'
that's neither, nor, if that, or there

your host for tonight is, name a name
what is wrong with the clap button?
did we ran out of cellophane?
again?
run the file of rain,
it's the same as clapping
twiddle on the volume knobs to make it real

focus on that one, he's doing something
he picks his nose
exactly,
he's brave enough to do it
he's doing something unique,
film it, home in, closer
get much closer into the thought absorbing,
deep down exploratory nose-pick event,
this, the world needs to share

what happened?
a bank collapsed, the mine-shaft's flooded,
her husband's underground,
how long ago? six hours
he surely must be dead

johnny, close up, get the waterfall,
we sell emotion,
squeeze each precious drop,
despair, tomorrow's stuffed,
she runs, run with her
get it all, drama sells, get all.

Mademoiselle Jane

Rescued from the Chain

Oh dearest Jane, where art thou, where?
Thy Pierre is pregnant with despair.
Do English hold thee in their prison?
Their Prince wants thee with lusting eyes.

Be true to thee be true to me,
I hope chastising belt will hold
and for our sake, swallow the key
until I rescue thee.

And if he asks for your submission
give him long finger from hand's mid,
laugh loud and grace him with a spit
and know thy Pierre will throw the Prince
into the deepest pit of ...
pardon, French passion as inferno flames.

Commissioned are three frigates,
a schooner and ten thousand men.
I sail the 'Ragamuffin',
and shall surround all the island's lands,
to search to find my gal's Jane chains
and get the Prince to eat them.

Will carry on my stallion thee
return to Ireland to be free.

To four green fields where clover grows,
the heather blooms and thyme,
where songs are sung, poetry read
and Jane's gift in the words she says,
'Oh Pierre, I'm yours, be mine.'

Millions of Frenchmen stand behind,
hear maiden's soft spoken request
and in one voice 'cross channel's waves,
"Pierre, hear her heart, say 'oui'"

'Oui, oui, my Lady Jane, but how?
You're all locked up, what do we do?'
'Be back in a wee moment, quick,
help me to find a loo,' says she.

Upon return the belt no more,
'And since you came from foreign shore'
oh Pierre, to rescue me,
no door be ever locked to thee',
says she, and he could see
the heaven smile

And every Frenchmen, mon amour,
ran to the cherry trees,
and each blew gently butterflies
that all around you see, chéri

your Pierre
in agonising wait for sign of life of thee

9.Dec 2008

Lassie Jane

Oh, Lassie Jane
tell me
Answer, please
No moments left,
each speaks your name

Rescue
Your Pierre
Abate his heart's aching brame
needless in pain, say 'oui'

Oh, Lassie Jane, a poet's fantasy,
a poem itself as never be
None knew the power in your name
Except your Pierre who goes insane,
Jane on his brain, since first he heard it said

Reminiscing days that not yet born, you met,
your arms reach out his breath to stop
As he saw you, his legs gave in and he dropped dead.
Yet you revived him with a kiss
Now look at him, with peaceful grin in dreamless bliss,
he's breathing in your name

Oh Jane, Jane oh
and lie I would
no nicer name
has ever chanced to near such gifting treasure to my ear;
euphoric sweet sonata's all I hear

Reserve,
your heart
and you will hear
no other name but Pierre

Oh, Jane, let's lose all our dreams.
and live instead a life of dreams.
Now while we can on earth
We start until we reach the heavens.

You lift me up, and I lift you.
and if the angels bless and guard our flight
Nirvana, Eden, Shangri-La, or Paradise
all in the fire of our eyes.

7. Dec 2008

flowers from a field

I took a flower from a field
to give to you
to let her whisper

she was asked the greatest sacrifice
and yes she went
a martyr now —

but in her time of glory
did you hear her whisper
see her shine
inhaled her scent and looked at her

and did she touch you inside
did she make you smile
and did she fill your heart
and will you still remember her

she could have done no more
as she did everything i asked
yet if you're filled with sorrow
if you grieve her passing

forgive me then
i had no right to cut her down
no right to use her beauty
yes if it grieves you let me know

8march86l

she speaks in whispers

she does not talk – but speaks in whispers
she'll use a language all her own
her words are beauty itself
she has no ears
but she can surely hear your thoughts

oh yes i know – this flower's dying
but so will we in time
she could die lonely in a field
no one would ever know she was

but now she is still blooming
she pleased the bees and butterflies
yes her greatest moment now
as she shines for your attention

she'll give her scent
and light her colours
yes she will glow seeking your attention
she'll try to shine for long

is not the knowledge
that you shared her time of beauty
reward enough

she shan't ask for more
except for water

take part in her time of glory
spare her a moment with a smile
she shared with bees and butterflies
and now is called to share with you
part of her life

oh yes the colours will fade
and the leaves will wither
but not today - not yet

and when her leaves have dropped
the colours faded — the scent long gone
is she not still glowing in your heart

and when the stem looks bare and sorry
her time of glory gone
your heart could make her shine
much longer than she ever would

oh yes — she's dying
and so shall we in time
but while she shines
just watch and listen

no,
i don't like
plastic flowers

march86
dm f ¦ g a#¦

somewhere

somewhere grows a flower
hidden in the shade
it may never show it's colours
'cause it's standing in the shade

somewhere is a garden
it may never grow
in the middle of a desert
where the rain won't dare to go

somewhere is an eagle
which did never fly
it's been trapped inside a cage
it has never seen the sky

somewhere is a dolphin
caught inside a cave
and it don't know how to get out
it may never catch a wave

every flower needs the sunshine
every garden needs the rain
every eagle needs a mountain
every dolphin needs a wave

C G am F C F G | |: 79

flowers grown a year ago

flowers grown a year ago
still leave their scent behind
with colours shining
in the dawn
no eye can see but mine

flowers grown a year ago
can never really die
one flower though
which never grew
still wonders through my mind

5jan80 caloundra I

just one as us

oh no your beauty never fades
it blossoms endlessly
and as your heart reflects
the depth of our love

so shines your eyes
rewarding every moment

no you
no me
just one as us

fuer immer
11march86 m|f a c e| f g b d

Rose of Hope

two years in search for rose of hope
each day eyes failed to find
until a summer's moonlit night
showed where you grew

one week, oh precious rose of hope
your scent dared me to dream
but then you shed your petals all
a thorny stick
I was left to hold

two years I held a barren stick
from it no rose did grow
and then it broke and flew away
never seen again

so now I dream of seven days
when I held rose of hope
with hilled heart 'n joy of promise feel
the pain each petal had to bear

it's pain I share
in sightless stare
wonder what could have been

5.Nov 2008

a passing dream

music echoes through the glen
trees silently listening
leafs touched
by whispering charm
moved in a passing dream

swallow flies within the waves
showered in reflections
absorbing some
slowly ceasing
caught to live again

dissolve to form and change
rising once more to grow
revived to search
for one embrace
dying to regenerate

6feb80 brisbane
am g c|f c| f c dm G ||:

What's it all about

Well, you my friend, you're trying hard
to make me believe in your good Lord
But I'm not sure what it's all about, can you tell me
I just don't know what is it all about

Well friend, I'm searching for a reason
I don't know why we're here at all
Why do we live, why am I asking, can you tell me
What is the sense behind it all

I can't accept your words like that
I've not been touched by what you've said
Can't hear no voice within my mind
can't see the light I tried to find

C G am D G || 06.77

Nothing you can keep forever

There's nothing you can keep forever
always a chance it could be gone
that's how it was and how it'll be
you cannot change it nor can anyone

A live-long of a loyal love
from a dog where there ain't no second off
it's still so nice when he licks your hand
but it all can change, he could lie dead in the sand

In a warm fur you need not be cold
if you don't take care it could be stolen
You build a house together with friends
but it could collapse or be eaten by flames

It was always so in this world
you can never say: protect me with gold
even the one you call your best friend
he can change that you'll never know him again

There's nothing you can keep forever
always a chance it could be gone
that's how it was and how it'll be
you cannot change it nor can anyone

translation from German: 66 Kassel / 17.04.78 Red Hill

Are we the ones?

Are we the outcasts from the stars
the rejects of the universe
the breed which never could be changed
the beasts which on this planet rages

This is the sad story of men
who has, what he calls the biggest brain
who learned to crawl, to walk and climb
began to swim, to dive and fly

We've made this world a different place
now trying to reach the outer space
we close our eyes and hide our face
as not to see the mess we've made

We've been 'round here just for a while
and guilty of the biggest crimes
we're changing nature every day
regardless of the cost to pay

Look at ourselves, see what we are
we take and grab and think that's smart
and we go hunting just for fun

and most of our culture's gone

And we have trained ourselves as slaves
and we've put numbers on the days
tried to perfect the human race
dumped the dead in monster graves

Given the order we will kill
and let the hard rain fall until
there's nothing left of us no more
and that will be the end of all,
are we the ones

am G F E||: am F E || C G am G, Feb 78, Feb 80

Beautiful land

Beautiful land, wonderful town
and sunrise at the Pacific Ocean
quiet streets, sleeping dogs,
only the dairyman about his business

Gradual awakening of life,
the children go to their school
and the train moves across the bridge,
that's peace, simply like it is

Kind people, street sweepers,
everybody knows what to do
majestic sailing boat
in front of a gray warship

make more noise city, I beg you,
don't want to hear of bombs and war
Rain come and fall and blur my eyes
so I can't see the land of war

Barking dogs, mighty rocks,
shopping housewives at the corner

busy boys sell newspapers
and the first page thread of a theatre of war

Beautiful land, wonderful town
and sunset at the heart of the country
quiet streets, sleeping dogs,
only the lighthouse man does his job

em C em ex em C D G F C D G F C D, apprx 72

---

once i knew

once i knew where i was going
thought i knew where i would be
but that was a long time ago
such a long long time ago

once i was so certain
once i really felt secure
but that was a long time ago
such a long long time ago

once i knew all the answers
had no worry on my mind
but that was a long time ago
such a long long time ago

72/26feb83
em d am d em | |:

---

because of you

and the morning
was so much nicer
'cause of you

and the day
was that much brighter
'cause of you

and the nights
they were sheer magic
'cause of you

'cause of you

pacific hwy

---

did you

did you hear the river talk
did you listen what it said

was the voice it used of many sounds
as there are colours in the field

did you hear the waterfall
did you listen to the sea

and the rain poured from a passing cloud
quenching flowers in the field

did you hear the ocean talk
did you listen to the lake

and the creek even the smallest pond
don't they all tell you the same

---

did they tell about their way
from the spring up to the sky

and the joy it gave and of the pain
like the tears inside your eye

24feb82 sl.creek
am g c c am e am | |: c g am|am g c|am g c|am e am

the last one

oh mum the last one he was nice
brought you some flowers
gave me lollipops, so nice

oh mum the last one he was right
ask him to come again
and let him stay the night

oh if the last one comes again
ask him to close the door
to all the other men

oh mum the last one was ok
ask him to stay with us
never to go away

9march82
sl.creek
c | c am| f g dm g# | |:

---

silence

in isolation growing
away from actualities
free of haste
ignoring screaming clocks

raindrops which i don't feel
reflections on the water surface
which lets me wait

a bird that sings
not just for lovers
melody not forgotten
smiling about simple things

Approx 71

---

to say what is

words are inadequate sometimes
they come out wrong
are misunderstood
and fail to say
what can't be said

another language may keep the answer
no need of words
and clear it speaks

it says without words
what is
not should or would
or could be

yet still we try to call it by the words
we've learned

they are not meant for this
they cannot cope

they cannot match
but just distort
what should be left to grow

sometimes

sometimes
i'm alright
go to bed and sleep right
through the night

but i do appreciate you asking
but no really sometimes it's OK
for just a little while
it all seems to go away

and it comes back again
and seems so real so very important
and nothing i can do
will make it go away

but i do thank you for your smile
grateful for your concern
but words ain't gonna cure it

don't feel sorry don't feel blue

don't change for me
do what you do
time will sort it out somehow

19march86v

free loving's over

the lights still glitter to the sound
and the rhythm's still the same
they gathered here to be found
and it all looks just the same

and the guys still perv across the hall
and the birds do just the same
and most of them are out to score
and they think it's just a game

but then prince charming never shows
so what's the use to wait
if the message doesn't get across
you'll be left behind for dead

and your mum cries every evening
and your dad don't understand
they're out of touch and anyway
they just wouldn't comprehend

your free loving is now over
'was never loving from the start
and it wasn't free that you know now
and i know it is damn hard

the lights still glitter in the dark
you can't see them anymore
they're still perving across the hall
and most are out to score

and the virgin-looking faces smile
and give the big 'come on'
and don't see what it's all about
until they're done and gone

the midnight queen is still choosing
something better for tonight
she'll spend the night with someone
and she will forget the name

but for you the rage is over
and the price you paid is high
all caused by a little loneliness
and the comfort of a night

free loving is now over
it was never loving from the start
and it wasn't free that you know now
and i know it is damn hard

and for you the rage is over
and the price you paid is high
all caused by a little loneliness
and the comfort of a night

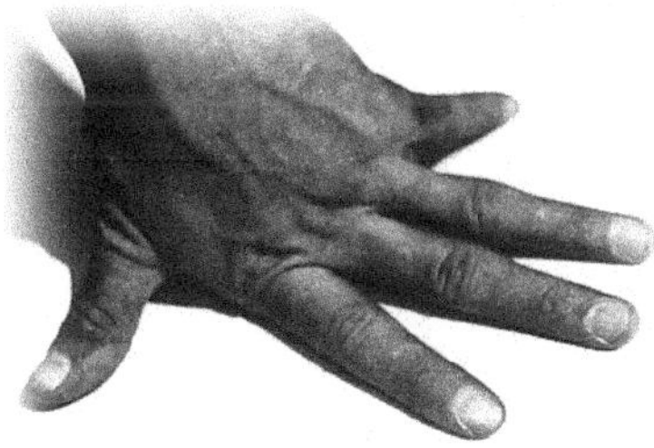

gm f c | a# f c gm7 ||

You're going

And now you're going
a long, long way down south
my thoughts are with you
everywhere you go

you know i'll miss you
miss your laughter and your smile
miss the many funny faces
and the tear inside your eye

take your time with growing
and learn your lessons well
relax and take it easy
take good care of yourself

deep within you is a garden
if you search you'll find the gate
to see the multicoloured flowers
feel the magic of the place

always there to be your refuge
pick you up when you feel down
and wherever you may wonder
always there to be your home

there's so much i want to tell you
still so much that you need to know
wish you find the answers
how i wish you find them all

10sep84 brisbane g d em c | |

learn how to fly

your eyes say i don't want to
but you know you have to try
still sitting on my hand now
you want to learn to fly

you clean your feathers gently
as if to gain a little time
you spread your wings out slowly
sadness is in our eyes

you left my hand you're flying
your wings still touch the ground
i hide the tears i'm crying
somewhere so they can't be found

you fly 'round in a circle
as if to say: so long
my eyes are going with you
watching until you're gone

i realise now that you've left me
i saw you fly away
somehow i can't believe it
wish you were here to stay

you fly across the mountains
heading towards the sea
you fly beyond the ocean
but wherever you will be

you'll know i am still standing
i hold my hand up high
i'm waiting for your landing
once you've learned how to fly

you'll know it when you're gliding
somewhere all alone
you'll remember I'm still standing
and my hand will be your home

then you'll fly across the ocean
and head toward the sea
you'll fly over the mountains
to the place 'we used to be

you'll fly 'round in a circle
as if to say: hello
my eyes are going to sparkle
watching every move you do

you'll glide down slow and easy
until you feel my hand
somehow you look exhausted
couldn't find no place to land

then your eyes say, i don't have to
ever say good bye
you're sitting on my hand now
and you've learned how to fly

You'll clean your feathers gently
each one at a time
you fold your wings in slowly
and peace is in your eyes.

d a bm f#m g d a ||:
06, 79

ask the birds

ask the sparrow, ask the robin
ask the blackbird, ask the owl
have they seen somewhere a dove
with golden legs

ask the parrot, ask the wagtail
ask the peewee, ask the finch
have they seen somewhere a dove
with golden wings

ask the lorikeet, the magpie
ask the hummingbird, the quail
have they seen somewhere a dove
with golden eyes

ask the nightingale, the pelican
ask the seagull, ask the hawk
have they seen somewhere a dove
that couldn't fly

ask the albatross, the eagle
ask the cranes, ask the stork
have they seen a dove
somewhere at all

25june79 brisbane
dm em || c dm em

i love you

i love you
you know i really do
ain't no word in the whole world
to express what i feel for you

i love you
with everything i do
no matter what i touch
you'll see that i love you

i love you
this song is just for you
please smile at me and close your eyes
to show you love me too

i love you
got nothing more to say
and if i sang 1000 songs
they all would say the same

i love you

C Cx am F C || C Cx am G F G 05.79

You closed the door

You closed the door, you're gone
you walked down the stairs
caught the first train leaving town

You see the city flying by
you don't even know
if that train will ever stop again

You light a smoke, put it out,
it doesn't make no sense

didn't see the children standing by the door

Oh yes, that train keeps rolling on
but it won't sing a song
it has an empty boring sound all the way

When you wake up you will know
where you have to go
there will be a jet waiting there for you

And you will see the ones around you
give everyone a smile
and you will know where you need to go

There will be a cup waiting, a flower right beside
and in the kettle water's boiling on the stove

C G F C | am D G | | 06.79

---

alice

there's a flower growing
in the middle of the desert

she's got such a pretty name
she's called 'alice'

keep on growing alice
make a field out of the desert

one day i'll come to see you
want to watch you grow

10july79brisbane
g c d g em g c d

clouds

the clouds rose up this morning
to paint the grass from the sky
they asked all sorts of questions
about the green inside your eye

the depth, how deep,
the light, how bright
which shade of hue
to find in you

i said i didn't know it
i never seen her eye
they said, how can we draw the grass
and hope to get it right

10may07 goldcoast

melody

oh melody, what will you be
a serenade for lovers
an opera or a symphony
the call of parent plovers

oh melody, what will you be
the sunshine in the shadow
a joy in dreamlike harmony
a rainbow in the meadow

oh melody, what will you be
a sound ever so pleasing
a lyrebird with every voice
little coy but also teasing

oh melody, what will you be
a tune so soft and soothing

or rock'n'roll and rhapsody
or the song of sperm-whales cruising

oh melody, what will you be
still full of unknown mystery
oh will you be the one for me
reality or fantasy

oh melody, what will you be
for me

18may07 goldcoast

I am a garden

please come inside I am a garden
do you know who I am?
the coloured leaves the diamond python
that is who I am

the singing bird — the sleeping possum
even the grass on which you stand
the bright reflection and the whistle
and the soil inside your hand

i am the dove and the pigeon
and the seagull in the sand
and the roses and the pebbles
and the algae in the pond

smell the blossoms, drink the water
taste the honey on your hand
please stay awhile I am a garden
you know who I am

em C||: June 79

---

southport flowers (Trigger warning: Loss)

surf's still great the guys are laughing having fun
and the sunrise clear as always been before
the girls are looking pretty and it's just a pity
but i think you would have liked them now

another summer has come and gone
surf is still OK as life goes on
the guys still laughing
nothing much has changed at all

except the young ones starting sooner
they try anything for kicks
and yeah they're tough and brave
and someday join you too

and in southport flowers wither on your plot
yesterday's headline is still OK for fish'n'chips
no mum to weep no dad to cry
not even 16 when you died
nothing at all is left behind of you

and the back-streets and the avenues
have seen the blood of many kids
on the surface all deceiving
for the dollar and the quids

and you know the goofy-footed kid
he used to go swimming off the spit
he got stoned right off his block
drowned just behind the rock
he's gone

there are no headlines anymore
i suppose it all becomes a bore
it's just another kid
that didn't make it

another summer has come and gone
surf is still good
but the waves aren't meant for you no more
the kids are laughing having fun
just like you used to be back then

ain't still no reason nothing new
just because something to do
and in southport flowers wither on your plot

and in southport flowers wither on your plot
yesterday's headline still OK for fish'n'chips
no mum to weep no dad to cry
not even 16 when you died
nothing at all is left behind of you

Video link: https://youtu.be/6PV1O9_j2dE

dec85, for billy

high-rise shadows

now the new high-rise throw their shadows in the sand

remember times when in the sun
surfing and girls were all the fun
we ever wanted out of life
somehow it changed
to something else

used to go cruising pick up chicks
and fooled around just for kicks

somehow the guys have changed in time
maybe they just have grown out of it
they settled down having kids and wife
and happy ever after

don't like the many faces gone
and new ones coming all the time
there must be something 'bout this place
that draws them in like flies

oh girl go back hit the track
this ain't meant for you at all
yeah you're confused and you'll be used
get so abused you won't even know it

and you try this and you try that
one day you wish you never had
many still come and hear the call
and when they're down here and they fall

they're oldies wonder what went on
and asking questions and so on
once was enough to ride the wave
fall in the sand and feel the breeze

did all the glamour and the show
somehow affect us ? well i don't know

and now the young they know it all
and if they make it well that's alright
but they have eyes to see who's missing
don't they? don't they

now the new high-rise throw their shadows in the sand

dec85

couldn't catch the time

i saw a friend today in town
last saw him a few years ago
and we were talking about ourselves
and all the things we used to do

showed me a picture of his children
and said that he had lost his wife
and I had made a thousand photos
but I just couldn't catch the time

72, Berlin

where are you

drove the highways
and the back streets
looking for you

went through the high class joints
and the honky tonks
trying to find you

from the supermarkets
to the corner store
no sign of you

where are you
where are you

nothing's changed

and here we meet again
not knowing what to say
your voice still makes me tingle
with every word you say

it's been so long you know
so long

wondering how you've changed
not knowing where you've been
always thought about you
forever now it seems

it's been so long you know
it's been so long

and here you're standing now
your eyes still shine and glow
and nothing's changed at all
nothing at all

the way i feel for you

dec85

just one germ

just one germ allowed to grow
could kill us all
but we can never really die
we will be again once more

maybe you will be the sun
in another galaxy
maybe i'll be inside a piece of dust
many light-years away

we come closer all the time
while we move away
eventually we'll meet again
and won't know what to say

we will talk with the light
no need of a sound

until we go on our way
in the circle 'round

9july79brisbane
hm em g || hm em a

Excitements

Running in the grass
running in the fields, and running

Steering down the track
as fast as it can get, and driving

Jumping off a cliff
hanging in the air, and gliding

Stuck inside the saddle
kicking with the heels, and riding

Kick-off in the match
diving for the catch, and going

Turning 'round and 'round
shaking to the sound, and dancing

Being close to you
making love with you, and smiling
touching, holding, feeling,
kissing, stroking, biting,
moving, scratching, breathing,
giving, living, exploding

hm G || A em, hm G f#m em | A, 04.07.97

Pretending

You're so close, yet still so far
wonder where you really are
can't you open up the door
and show me what's inside you

Right behind those clear, blue eyes
another world of mystery lies
how does one get close to you
how do I get to know you

    Talking about a million things
    but never saying what you think
    and when you talk you always smile
    inside you may be crying

Your body shows what you don't say
but always find another way
to cover up the things you feel
how come you don't get tired

The face you show is always kind
but who knows what's inside your mind
all those silly games we play
to keep us isolated

Talking 'bout a million things....

Hide behind your make-up smile
just like the clothes you're wrapped inside
pretend what you want to be
perhaps one day you'll see

break down the walls around yourself
and put away that dual face
and show me who you really are
that I may get to know you
am D am D C G am D em D G ... 14-17. Feb 80

The power of life

As conjoined twins,
one leaning,
as if to guard its sibling's south
to give it space,
to nurse its growth
clearing the way to light

towards the east
both greet the day
in illustrious show of splendour,
a sight of strength,
of reaching loft,
both equal, blend as one

few see twin's pain,
which from the west,
scorched cores,
mere shells at best,
each maimed, despite,
time grants no rest,
whilst force of life is feeding

and thus, all living's quest a must
unfold the gifts it's given,
bring honour to what's there to craft
shine glorious its deed

12th April 2010, Cape York

I give you everything

'Come with me, I give you everything.
I chase away the boy.'
She duly kept her promise;
At 12 he had it all.

Blind eye

What if one turns
The other way
Ignore what's there,
'Blind eye' they say,
Soon be no place to turn to.

2010, Cape York

Child's eye

child's eye a two-way mirror
reflecting some, absorbing all
all that goes in comes out
as sorrow or as shine

2010, Cape York

Let it out

don't hold it back
let it out
it won't bother you no more

can't always hide
behind the face of a cloud
it won't make it go away

i know sometimes
it is really hard
ain't no easy way in sight

it could even break your heart
with a little help
you will survive

don't hold it back
let it out
it won't bother you no more

3july79brisbane
f c || dm g

Still you are very small

Still you are very small
and you are happy to be with me
but it won't be long and you'll be tall
and you look at me differently

So my child, I want you to know
I'll understand your ways
and I will always love you
even though you might not love me

And I pray, that I can show you
my love day by day

for Larsen

For your life

this is the morning of your life
it's the time to grow and treasure
and everything is right
make this the best time of your life

and comes high noon of your life
it's the time you see your seeds grow
and everything is right
it'll be the best time of your life

and comes the evening of your life
when you'll reflect on your memories
and you'll know everything was right
it'll be the best time of your life

for Larsen

Can't think of no pretty words

Can't think of no pretty words
which to say to you
but when I look into your eyes
you'll know that I love you

please forgive me if I don't
bring you flowers everyday
but you know that I love you
with every word I say

Let desire bloom

got together with my woman tonight
did a lot of talking, made me feel alright
glass of scotch, soft candle light
gentle voice and dreamy eyes

you move me with your romantic smile
let me drink from your sweet wine
lead me to your room
let desire bloom

The string

I'm only a string with lots of knots, help me
I once was a ball but I'm really a string, help me
I'm only a jumper but I can't jump
it's lonely without a kid inside
all around I'm knit but inside need a kid
it's cold without a kid inside

Life is

Life is, accept it,
used to ask why
but I couldn't find a reason
or sense behind

I am, that I know,
'cause I'm alive and here
and I see and taste,
feel and smell and hear

Life is, accept it,
never ask why
if you knew what Life is
you still need to live it

If you knew what air is
you still need to breathe it
so you know, Life is,
why don't you just live it

pre 1980

Your time will come one day

your time will come one day
'til then just stay
but read again two lines above
what does it say

your time will come one day
what does it mean
the line that says
your time will come one day

it's not the end, that day
the day you think of is
when all the time has gone away

your time will come one day
just means the day you're born
as time is at your side each day
until it goes away

no need to seek the man with scythe
turning green growth to hay
he's got his spot along the way
he shall find you and say

your time has gone away
'til then enjoy the day

4.Apr.2008

Words said to Joe

Could I suggest, raising your head,
out of the shame instead?

Instead, ahead is she, the one that fills your book
with words, eventually.

What if you knew, the view would not be so, at 93.
The words to be, is it not `she',
not then, but 'now', she, you can see?

Joe, see her for the first time ever,
as vision never seen before.
The time you can is now, not then, at 85, or more.

The pain in tow, let go, to mind its own affair.
Give history its share and let it stare.

So squeeze the pain out of the sponge
and watch it drip away.

The eye of her can light the tunnel bright.
She streams as runnel, fills your funnel,
if you let her in.

Absorb her essence, gist of gifts,
none draining, paining, staining.

Wonder of life a treasure,
no math able to measure.

So let her shine inside,
not in the brain that's thirsting.
Soak her gifts, invite into your whole of self.

Sense with your ears, your nose, your eyes,
your skin, your taste and all your being,
being near, being dear,
being without any fear.

And speak in any sounds you choose,
as everything she does will soothe,
if you're aware that she is breathing
right there, Joe, in front of you,
and deep within.

Two, three, as four, a little more,
no number key to unlock door
that she can be, as light.
No number can kiss Joe 'goodnight'.

Numbers with life are none,
except the number 1,
and then it's spelled as 'one',
the 'one' you know by name.

No digit ever speaks a sound,
none will have scent,
or breast that's round,
none anywhere, but one.

All digits one can analyse,
manipulate, categorize,
yet all are dead or paralysed,
except the one with eyes.

Something equals something else,
but nothing equals her,
without, nothing is right.
None will be bright, as all are shells.

A `drama' with a lovely wife,
how can that be, Joe? Be.

Don't mean to step on toe of Joe.
Joe may not want to know,
he didn't ask.

If that is so, forgive me, Joe,
the now of now will pass
and so will time.

29.10.2007

Our highest treasure

to my friend whose heart is broken
let me tell you through your pain
that love is still the highest gift that we can share

yet you will never know
for how long it will stay
will never know if and when it calls again

so taste your tears and lick your wounds
they won't hurt forever
but while they do appreciate
how fragile love can be

do not get bitter from the pain
don't let it break you down
but feel it, yes, and let it help you grow

start from the now and climb a step
give yourself a chance
do not forget her and don't curse her
but keep what was dear once

and may love be our highest treasure
sometimes it's not enough
learn to listen, learn to hear
and listen then to what you hear
and feel and feel what others feel
and with every little pain you'll grow
life just prepares you for the next step

and if you still feel down and out
things only can get better
maybe in another way as you may hope for now
but maybe more rewarding in the long run

Play the numbers

20 ifs and 30 maybes
not even be one yes or no
40 are not really certain
50 more just don't know

60 are still undecided
70 are not sure
80 more can't make their minds up
90 don't know what it's for

well mister you can play the numbers
add them all up and then divide
subtract a few and carry over
to the left and to the right

200 ifs, 300 maybes
not even be one yes or no
400 are not really certain
500 more just don't know

600 are still undecided
700 are not sure
800 more can't make their minds up
900 don't know what it's for

well mister you keep playing numbers
use them in any way you like
as long as they remain just numbers
nothing happens, you'll be right

2000 ifs, 3000 maybes
not even be one yes or no
4000 are not really certain
5000 more just don't know

6000 are still undecided
7000 are not sure
8000 more can't make their minds up
9000 don't know what it's for

well mister you're still playing numbers
still adding up and then divide
somehow it gets a little harder
they're getting bigger all the time

2 million ifs, 3 million maybes
may not even be one yes or no
4 million are not really certain
5 million more just don't know

6 million are still undecided
7 million are not sure
8 million more can't make their minds up
9 million don't know what it's for

well mister keep on playing numbers
use them whichever way you like
but never turn them into people
then they may haunt you 'til you die.

june79 brisbane, gm d

Only one day

our history is filled
with pain blood and sorrow
tragedies of our past
our fear for tomorrow

so we fight for our ideals
and fighting we fall
and we honour our heroes
and for vengeance we call

and it only counts to win
for whatever reason
the opponent is wrong
and that's why we have to beat them

if every man in every nation
thought that way
oh brother, where are we heading?
there's got to be another way

if there only would be one day
when we are friends
only one day when we would be together
a day when we could talk and think

a day when we wouldn't be hostile
a day of liberty for all humanity
a day of catholics, of moslems and jews
a day of protestants, of hindus and all faiths

a day of communism and of socialism
a day of democracy and liberalism
a day of any colour of the skin
a day of all faces a day of kind

a day of children of youth and of the old
a day when all nations be united
a day without borders
with a worldwide common feeling

a day of joy of love and peace
a day of trust and tolerance
a day we shouldn't fail
to let it happen

March 80

Mother don't wait

oh mother, please don't wait for me
don't wait for me tonight
oh mother, i have gone
i won't be back tonight

somebody, i don't know who
but someone threw a bomb
it did explode beside my head
and that is how i've gone

please do not cry and stop your tears
and you don't have to pray
oh mother can you hear my voice
then listen what i say

i know that you have lost a son
and this time it was me
but 1000 sons have died this year
1000 times like me

please mother go and get my gun
and all the guns you see
and all the tanks and cannons
throw them into the sea

and tell my brother not to shoot
or touch another gun
for i won't live and he shan't kill
another mother's son

there are a million mothers
a million times in pain
take care of the next you grow
he not be killed again

my mother lives in belfast
hanoi, jerusalem
lives in saigon and in phnom penh
in any town you name

1945

it must have been a good day back in 1945
when the war was over and you were alive
and on that day in 1945 you didn't load your gun
that's when they finally surrendered
it's all over now, it's done

maybe your father killed, your sister raped
your brother missing, your mother dead
you full of pain – but you survived

those crying children
screamed for years inside your mind
the vision of dead bodies
wouldn't let you sleep at night
your broken youth took long to heal
you tried hard to forget
the stinking smell, the noise, the smoke
the dying mates, the hand grenade

but it all keeps coming back
the concentration camps, the bones
the cut-off heads and bloody guts
and starving men in overcrowded camps

and you were there to see it all
to see the ruins of the war
you saw how ugly men can be
but you survived
but life goes on and time helps covering your scars
and it was over then, it was all over
they said: 'we must never forget'
and that we always should remember

and let us never fight again
oh let us never fight again
never ever fight again

well, that was many years ago
before korea and vietnam
and bangladesh and cambodia
and cyprus and israel
and laos and ireland
and pakistan and egypt
and jordan and syria
and lebanon and angola
and timor and rhodesia
and algiers and ethopia
and zaire and biafra
and congo and nicaragua
czechoslovakia and india
afghanistan and ...
and ...
and ..
and .
and
iran, el salvador, libya, beirut, sinai, falklands, india, palestine,
malaya, suez, kenya, borneo, aden, radfan, oman, dhofar, gulf,
kosovo, sierra leone, solomon is, bosnia, somalia, kuwait, Iraq...

Video: https://www.youtube.com/watch?v=4G0Wr5fpE90

29/30march78 red hill, am g f c am em||

---

ww

and in the end they all say "no, "I didn't do it"
they act surprised as if to say "I never knew it"
ain't 1 and 2 enough?

Truckie's nightmare

fourteen hours on the track
jackie beaver hits the sack
and in his sleep he has a dream
the most awful one he'd ever seen

it was about a certain load
which had to go through a certain road
and this here road led to a town
without a detour – no way 'round

and this here town all truckies know
that's why they didn't want to go
well then they settled for a draw
to see who's going to move the load

jackie beaver had no luck
they all start laughing but he said f_ck
well jackie moved that certain load
900 miles to a certain road

it's the sunday driver town
yeah sunday driver town ||:

the word spread quicker than the sound
a truck is on its way to town
even the preacher stopped to pray
there is a truck coming our way

It's time to give the cars a shine
get all dressed up and get some wine
and everybody running 'round
as jackie beaver comes to town

they got the picnic on the way
with scones and cream and marmalade

and kids were dancing men drank beer
hoping that truck will soon be here

the road was filled with cars and bikes
everyone driving as they liked
and the band sings out loud
jackie beaver comes to town

to our sunday driver town
yes the sunday driver town ||:

then news got out that out of bound
10 miles away there is a sound
jackie beaver and his load
driving along a certain road

and this here road leads to a town
without a detour – no way 'round
and this here road all truckies know
that's why they didn't want to go

it's the sunday driver town
yeah the sunday driver town ||:

as jackie saw the gathered crowd
his face turned pale and sweat broke out
that's when he woke up from his dream
the most awful one he'd ever seen

about a sunday driver town
yes a sunday driver town ||:

then jackie drove along a track
into a town when he really woke up

THIS is the sunday driver town
will you look at this
did you see that

watch it mate
oh for crying out loud

4march82 sl.creek

---

poet's words forgotten

the poet's words forgotten
as the pages catch the flames
and the painters canvas peeling
colours fading all is stained

the teachers age in disbelief
turn their faces and cry
one time goddess fantasize
'til she rejoins with a sigh

so the idols dance like puppets
like the new in vain
to each its time of glory
as to each its time of pain

and the plastic generation falls
as the new will yet again
trapped in rhythmic cycles
intervals dictating now

back to what i thought
i'd left behind

About the author

Welcome to the vivid tapestry of the author's artistic voyage. From an early age, he proclaimed his destined course as a writer, hinting at the extraordinary journey that lay ahead. Alongside his passion for music creation, he explored the visual arts and video production, broadening his creative horizons and nurturing an enduring quest for artistic discovery.

His musical compositions became transcendent channels for emotions, freed from linguistic confines, as books, akin to vessels, became conduits for his thoughts, dreams, and explorations across a diverse range of creative paths.

From poetry to articles, from magazine production to his diverse array of books, compositions, and videos, the author's unwavering passion for artistic expression shines through. Within the pages of his works, readers are welcomed to embark on an extraordinary voyage where inspiration intertwines with imagination, prompting thought-provoking questions along the way.

heinzross.com

No art, and all would fall apart.